MISSISSIPPI

is a collection of 77 poems

from

Nights Under A Tin Roof

and

Life After Mississippi

by

James A. Autry

MISSISSIPPI

Nights Under a Tin Roof
and
Life After Mississippi

by

James A. Autry

Yoknapatawpha Press
OXFORD, MISSISSIPPI

Copyright 2018 by James A. Autry

Published by Yoknapatawpha Press, P.O. Box 248, Oxford, MS 38655

Printing history:

> *Nights Under A Tin Roof (1983)*
> *Life After Mississippi (1989)*

ISBN 978-0-916242-86-2

Printed in the United States of America

Book Layout and cover design by Chad Murchison

CONTENTS

Chapter IV - Worship

Chapter V - Death

FOREWORD

When I first read some of these pieces to a fellow Mississippian, a writer now living in Virginia, she said, 'I'm astonished that you look back with such benevolence, with no bitterness."

It was then I realized I was not sticking to the mode of the expatriate Southerner who tends to pass judgment on "the magnolia mentality" or to scorn the southern social structure.

Well, I thought, there's nothing I can add to what's been said already. And if there were I still wouldn't do it here. Not in these recollections, because they were not seen with the adult eye or filtered through the sensitivities of the educated. All that stuff came later, found its way into prose now tucked under papers in old college footlockers or into speeches made in the sixties and seventies.

Instead, here are the forties and fifties, not as an examination of forces shaping the South, rather as forces shaping me. Personally. Just me. Mississippi boy, adolescent, teenager.

Maybe I'll take my turn at all that professional southern introspection one of these days. Certainly it's in me, but it would not be, were there not also a nurturing presence from an earlier, gentler time.

I suppose I've needed for many years to express that earlier time in a form which could somehow paint the place and character and people and language with the generosity and gratitude I feel. But until 1977 I was unable to come even close to doing it.

Then I heard James Dickey reading from his own work one evening; it was so powerful, so full of what I wanted to create that I returned to my hotel and scribbled seven short poems before the night was over. They were terrible but represented a change of form and, more important, a change in my thinking. For that I thank James Dickey, whose work sets a wonderful standard for us all.

I'm not sure my early poems were poetry, and some people have asked if the work in this book is really poetry. Each reader can answer for himself. I call these writings "pieces" because their shape comes to me as stories and then as pieces of a larger story.

Their form began to emerge in 1980 when Betty Sue Flowers, friend and mentor, scholar, professor, and poet, took it upon herself to help my understanding of, thus my writing of, poetry. We met at the Aspen Institute in 1980, and Betty Sue has carried on a mostly long-distance seminar with me ever since, a gift I can never repay.

As for making a book, the thought never occurred to me until late one night in Oxford, Mississippi, when I ended up at the faculty house of Willie Morris who, at the time, was writer in residence at Ole Miss. He read one of his essays, later to be published in Terrains of the Heart.

"Your turn to read something," he said, much to the disappointment, I'm sure, of a couple of students who had been swaying with his every word. I had some poems in my briefcase, and after I read two, Willie pointed to me and said, "Come home, Autry. Come home and publish."

That late-night performance led to a meeting with Larry Wells who listened to a few poems, read others for himself, then wrote a letter saying he would like to publish a book of my poetry. Soon after, I met his wife, Dean Faulkner Wells who told me that my work reminded her of her childhood near Oxford. Then it unfolded, as these spiritual connections seem always to do, that several of these poems were written about the same places, the same people, the same church experiences–for her grandfather (mentioned by name in one poem) and my father were songleader and preacher, respectively, in the same church at the same time.

By my romantic vision, that coincidence makes this book a project of the spirit. Nothing less.

Throughout it all, I have been supported by loved ones, family and friends too numerous to list. But I love you all and I thank you all.

A few words about the photographs. They come from three sources: the Library of Congress, the Mississippi Department of Archives and History, and family photo albums. These pictures are here to complement and not specifically to illustrate the poetry; enjoy them as another artistic expression of many of the same themes and events.

J.A.A.
Van Meter, Iowa 1983

INTRODUCTION
by John Mack Carter

New York, N.Y. November 1, 1982

When I first came north many years ago to work in New York City, I didn't understand how much I didn't know. I plunged into this new world happily and confidently, with no fear of the new experiences and no envy of any person. After a few months one of my new-made friends, a native New Yorker only a few years older but with a lifetime of metropolitan sophistication, confided, "I envy you. You know who you are." I recall that comment because I remember my puzzlement. I had always known who I was. Yet here was a woman who seemingly had the answer to every question about the city and its celebrities as well as a world across the ocean I hadn't even seen, yet she envied my native knowledge of self. This is why when Jim Autry told me he was writing these poems, I knew exactly what it was he was inspired to share with us. I suggest that this shared experience can be a thing of great value.

Jim and I have worked as contemporaries in the same profession of editing magazines. And we both have come the long way to New York to do it. But the instant I met Jim I knew that we were bound in a kinship that only could be formed by nights and days "under a tin roof."

Ours was a time of the South that produced writers, possibly because it was a time that promised to go on forever. We were living in an endless summer that owed nothing to tomorrow, and we were bound by neither urgency nor despair. The swollen sun was all the promise we needed.

Most of that South is gone, and the new South of progress and change–better in so many ways–may not provide these songs again.

For all of us lucky enough to know who we are, and those of us still eager to find out, Jim has laid this roof of tin.

Nights Under A Tin Roof

I. Rhythms

Photo courtesy of the Library of Congress

Nights Under a Tin Roof

I

When the fire still sends its yellow light from the bank of coals
is best
before the cold pushes us under the quilts
while the frost is still invisible in the air
And we can look up to the uneven planks fifteen years from the sawmill
and still not painted
and make things and faces in the wood grain
and be scared and laugh

> *You boys settle down in there*
> *We' ll be getting up 'round here*
> *in a few minutes*

But we wouldn't
as we didn't stop peeking the cracks at Allie Jo and Mae Beth

> *You see Allie Jo's pants*
> *You didn't neither*
> *Did too when she blew the lamp*

Peeking those same cracks that let the wasps through
that always needed stuffing with paper.

Uncle Virgil covered the kitchen cracks with wallpaper from the catalogue but
mice ate the wheat paste making tunnels like moles
and Uncle Vee mashed them with his fist and pulled them through
so the kitchen wall had little holes in the printed roses where a tunnel
stopped
And the rest of the rolls are wrapped in newspaper under the bed
because it might work better someday with another paste

> *Now you boys don't pee off the porch*
> *do your business under the chinaberry tree*

Those same cracks that let the smells through the floor
like the time Aunt Callie put out the ant poison and the rats got it on their feet
then licked them and died under the house

You ain't smelled stink till you smelled
a old wolf rat dead with the poison

And who had to rake them out with a stick
who was little enough to squeeze under the floor scared of snakes
and gagging with the smell

Take em yonder to the gulley boys
mind that lye on your hands

II

When the rain plays different notes
high near the peak and low in the middle
is best
When the thunder is far off down the Tippah bottom
and the wind is settled to breezes
and early before light we hear the back door and Uncle Vee's boots
and the pine fire in the stove and the lid on the salt box
and the pot boiling

Boys don't put so much sugar
in that coffee

But there was always the lightning when it struck the cat
right out of Jimmie Lee's arms and burned out the screen door
and killed the cat and only knocked Jimmie Lee down

Thank you Lord for that sign

And we can't go out in it especially under the trees
or go near the stove or windows

Stay on the bed and don't touch the floor boys
and don't bounce

and only the girls can use the slop jar except when it lightnings
and we always need it then

Well use the slop jar boys
but you'll have to take it out

When the dark comes with the afternoon clouds
and we hear lightning striking the pines on hickory nut hill
and the air whispers like God shushing everybody before the thunder
we try not to jump when it comes
and Aunt Callie brings tea cakes from the kitchen
round and sugary and crumbly with burned bottoms
and chewy with thick middles
and cow's milk to dip them

> *Don't drip on the quilt boys*

And Uncle Vee crumbles corn bread in blue john milk
and rocks and looks out the window

> *It'll be dry 'nough to pick up potaters boys*
> *if the lightnin' didn't scare the life*
> *outta preacher mule*

III

When a whip-poor-will sets in the yard and calls another in the garden
is best
and we sleep on top of the covers
when the windows are propped open
and balls of last year's cotton are wired on the screens with hair pins
keeping out the flies
And we hear Uncle Vee hiking there the walker hounds
to the bottom below the old place

> *Just listen at the window boys*
> *you'll hear the hounds good as me*

And Aunt Callie washes a block of ice from the sawdust pile
and puts it in a pitcher of cistern water

> *Don't play around that cistern boys*
> *we'll never see you again*

That's when the snakes come out
like the copperhead that bit Aunt Callie getting up the cows
and Uncle Vee tore his shirt for her heel
and we ran all the way to Cousin Verdell's who had a Dodge

Knowed somethin' was wrong boys
when I heard your feet slappin' the ground

When the night doesn't cool down
Uncle Vee puts his feet in a dishpan of water
and Miss Ann fans with the big palm leaf James Edward brought from Hawaii
before he got killed on the destroyer in the Solomons
after Becky won the Miss USS Edward Turner contest
and his dog Frisco just went off and died

    Let him go boys
    he don't want you to find him

Uncle Vee doesn't sell the place
but he'll let me put a house on it someday
with a tin roof

    Best roof in the world if you nail it right boys
    take a twister

And it keeps the place dry
and turns away the summer sun
and sends back the fireplace heat through the winter cracks
And holds everything together through the storms

Communication

Now we dial the phone
but Aunt Callie still yells into it
and ends every sentence with a question mark
as if she can't believe that all her words
can get through those little wires

But back then we stepped out and pointed our voices
across the hills

   Whooooeeee

It would follow the bottoms and up the next hill
and in a few minutes
it would come back from Cousin Lester

   Whooooeeee

When there was trouble
Uncle Vee would blow the fox horn
or ring the dinnerbell
and someone with a car would come
not knowing the problem but that we needed a car.

When Uncle Vee yelled or blew the horn
there was a message to send

   Don't you boys be out there
   yellin' up somebody
   'less you got somethin' they need to know

But we'd yell
and the old folks would know we were just yelling
and let it go
our high voices somehow falling short of the next hill
the dogs not even coming from under the porch.

Weeks would pass without a real yell
then it would roll up the hill from Cousin Lester's

Whoooooeeeeee

And Uncle Vee would step out on the porch
and cup his hands and answer
and turn his head and listen
nodding at the message I could never understand.

It's how we heard Cousin Lottie got snake bit and James Louis came back from the
Pacific
It's how the fox hunts were arranged and the hog killings set
They yelled about babies born and people cured
about fires and broken bones and cows loose and dogs lost the words always short
and spaced
for the distance they had to travel.

Now there are the wires
and Aunt Callie still yells for the distance and looks at the phone
holding it so her eyes can aim the words through the instrument and across the
hills where they are to go

Cotton Poison

We called it cotton poison
and its smell became good
drifting across the roads with the dust
lying in clouds on the July fields
Because underneath
we knew it was killing the weevil
and the weevil had killed us
every year before

Until the poison came
the cotton was armpit high and good
but inside the weevil was doing his work
Until the poison came
we carried barlow knives to the fields
and mashed the weevil from the split boll
hoping one hard death would scare the others
and heal the cotton
Until the poison came
it was God's will and the weevil was his

Now the poison drifts with the tractor dust
and the soldiers come home from Okinawa and the Bulge
ride into the night and jump in the river
the dust floating from their overalls
and laugh themselves dry
thinking of a bale to the acre
Because they beat the weevil like they beat the Nazis and Japs
and all their daddies could do was pray

The Snakes

There were snakes
my god there were bad snakes
but we didn't see all that many
except in Aunt Callie's imagination
under every log and in every brushpile

> *Now you chirren watch*
> *you'll step on a snake*

We knew them all
the copperhead/rattlesnake pilot/highland moccasin
(all the same snake)
plus the gentleman rattlesnake
who would always rattle before he struck
and the treacherous cottonmouth
hidden beside the path waiting for the chance to bite not run

> *Cottonmouths got to discharge that poison*
> *so they got to bite somethin' or somebody*

And there were copperbelties not poison but mean
and after Uncle Vee killed them
he pushed their heads into the soft mud with a stick
deep so half the snake was in the hole

> *It's a sign our family*
> *killed the snake*

And there were good snakes especially the king snakes

> *You ought to see him kill a bad 'un boys*
> *wrap hisself around that other'n*
> *and squeeze him to death*

But we killed them all
because a snake was a snake

Well I couldn't tell, Uncle Vee
they all look bad

There were spreading adders that puffed and hissed and acted mean
but couldn't hurt you
and rat snakes and bull snakes and hog nose snakes
and chicken snakes that ate our eggs and baby chicks
and when you reached into a nest on a high shelf in the chicken house
an old settin' hen might peck you

or it could be a chicken snake
so sometimes eggs in a high nest would go rotten
because we'd all think the next day's cousin would get them.

There were blue racers and black racers
and one time rabbit hunting
Uncle Vee and Cousin Lester saw a racer and kicked it
like when they were boys
and it curled up in a ball
and the other one kicked it high in the trees
it staying in a tight little ball
then both running for it and Cousin Lester kicking Uncle Vee
and they both falling in the leaves

Won't that kill the racer, Uncle Vee?
Sure will

And glass snakes that broke into pieces when you hit them
yes, really into sections
each one wiggling on its own

You leave him alone boys
he'll get back together
no matter how far you scatter them pieces
take one a mile away he'll get back together

One day on the path to the spring
Jimmy Lee and I saw a hog nose snake swallowing a toad
so we watched him do it
throwing his jaw all out of joint
the toad kicking his legs and hopping

making the snake's head jump off the ground
like a snake with hind legs in its head
then when the toad was inside
we killed the snake and cut him open
and the toad hopped away.

But the mean snakes were moccasins
even the un-poison ones
the brown water snakes at the swimming hole
that come toward you with open mouths hissing

> *They got a nest here somewhere boys*

and we always argued whether they could bite you under water
and we never found out.

After Aunt Callie got bit by the copperhead
all the men went hunting for bad snakes
with hoes and some shotguns
They turned over logs and whistled at brushpiles
saying a long straight whistle will bring them out
and at the end had killed hundreds of snakes
bad and good
and we measured the longest ones
and some of the boys skinned them for belts.

Then we didn't worry about snakes for a while
and hoped maybe they were all killed off

> *They'll be back boys*
> *they were in the Garden of Eden*
> *and they'll be back here*

Seasons Came with Food

I

Seasons came with food
not the other way around
certainly not with rain or winds or sun
or any weather at all
But when onion sets and potato cuts went in
it was February and the red sand soil
was cold under the fingernails
and our noses ran

> *Now you chirrun*
> *keep those coats buttoned*

Then it was mustard greens
we sowed in patches
to mix with wild poke salad
or collards that would take the frost.

When the water warmed we'd fish
for lazy willow cats hungry after the winter
or blues or jugheads or the quick channels
caught on set hooks and trot lines
run late at night in a boat
or barefoot along the slick bank
fighting mosquitos and scared of cottonmouths

> *Don't step over a log*
> *you can't see the other side of, boys*

Girls picked dewberries low on the ground
and somebody would make a pie

> *I declare you chirrun*
> *eat yourself sick*
> *if I let you*

Aunt Callie would can the rest
sweating over the steaming pots
with summer almost here
and the garden in and the greens up

> *A mess of greens and a pone of bread*
> *won't be long now*

Then it seemed something all the time
squash and new potatoes and green onions
the meals getting good and the canning hotter.

II

There came the day when
we soaked rags in coal oil
and tied them on our wrists and ankles

> *Them chiggers love blackberry bushes*
> *better'n I love blackberries*

And we'd fill our one gallon buckets
with the dark berries staining our hands
and chiggers getting past the coal oil
with the wasps nests and the yellow jackets
and always the snakes

> *Copperheads love to lie up*
> *in the shade of those blackberries*
> *so make plenty of noise chirrun*

Then everything was easier
with only some wild plums to pick
and potatoes turned over by a plow
looking rich and good in the dirt
and stored in piles in a dark place
under the house

> *Now don't you boys whine about spiders*
> *just mind your business and come back*

for another load
We ate peas and corn and tomatoes and
greens and onions and cornbread
and drank buttermilk
when the cows got into bitterweed
and the sweet milk tasted bad
And when everybody was full of watermelon
Aunt Callie made preserves from the rinds
and ground and chopped squash and cucumbers
and pickled little hot peppers
to pour over the greens and sop with bread.

III

By September the woods smelled of muscadines
and we picked them by the gallon
shaking trees and laughing when they rained on us
then finding them among the leaves

> *I declare you chirrun eat more*
> *than you put in the bucket*

Their seed sacks shot into our mouths
as we sucked the musky hulls
And Aunt Callie canned some and made jelly
and preserves and acid drink

> *Now I tell you that ain't wine*
> *and I don't want to hear no more about it*

and if we were good
fried pies crisp outside
where they almost burned in the skillet
and sometimes skim cream
to put on a cobbler
we'd eat in front of a young fall fire

> *You spoil those chirrun to death*

And we'd clean our guns

and talk about deer and rabbits and ducks and quail
and laugh at who'd miss
and who'd have to clean the rabbits

     Worse smell
     Lord I'd rather skin a skunk

Or Uncle Vee would get the smokehouse
ready for the hog killing

     Soon's we're sure the weather'll stay cold.

IV

Still later when ice was on the ponds
with the salt box full
and jars on the shelves
the colors of their contents tempting us
the comfort of it would settle upon us
and some morning soon after Christmas
before a pine fire
Uncle Vee would be looking out the window

     Think we'll put the potaters
     between the fruit trees this year boys
     mights well use that ground

then one day it wouldn't seem so cold
and we'd hear the gee and haw
and the chains on the single tree
and the soft tearing of the new ground
over the plow

After a season of planting and weeding and harvesting, a woman of Greene county, Georgia, shows off her canning and cupboard in 1941. Photo from the Library of Congress.

Left: Father and son sharpen their mower on a rainy day in Carroll county, Georgia, 1941.
Below: Father and daughter with a load of cotton in Alabama, 1933.
Right: Wearing a bonnet against the North Carolina sun, 1940.
Photo: Library of Congress.

Left and Right: Slopping the hogs, a daily chore leading to that inevitable time when a fat sow is killed and butchered. Photo: Mississippi Department of Archives and History, Florence Mars collection.
Below: Sorghum-making with a mule turning the mill. Photo: Library of Congress

Nothing defined life's rhythms so much as the growing season. Planting, tilling, weeding, and harvesting were the events which shaped life from the time the spring sun began to warm the soil. Here a Georgia farmer plows a garden with his mule while his son follows and carefully drops peas into the new ground. At right, a Mississippi farm hand chops cotton under a relentless sun.
Photos: Library of Congress

All over the south schools closed at cotton-picking time, and the children went to the fields, dragging their 11-foot sacks between the rows. The children at left were photographed in Arkansas in about 1940. Below, the cotton wagons gather at the gin in Clarke county, Georgia in 1940. Photos: Library of Congress. At right, voters in Mississippi consider the merits of keeping Jim. Photo: Mississippi Department of Archives and History, Florence Mars collection.

In between numbers they sipped moonshine or sucked at beer bottles then kicked off the beat for another tune. It happened in national guard armories and at street dances. The band at left is Cajun, playing for a fais-dodo in Louisiana. The street dancers are in the same town, circa 1938. Photos: Library of Congress. (Also overleaf) Below, Mississippi men gather on the square for first Monday business. Photo: Mississippi Department of Archives and History, Florence Mars collection.

Buzzards

I

Buzzards would stack
a hundred at a time
the highest fly specks in a hot summer sky
and circle something dead
And we'd wonder what it was
and talk about walking to it
through the woods
sighting on the stack of buzzards
until we'd arrive underneath
and there it would be
whatever it was
Dead and big
we knew it would be big

II

But we did it one time
making two buzzards fly
filling the air
with their awful smell
and it was only a rabbit
all those buzzards for one dead rabbit
Were they waiting their turn
up there a mile
turning turning never flapping a wing
not a feather
riding on some wind we couldn't see or feel
and waiting a turn
on one dead rabbit?
Were dead things in such short supply?

III

It was the depression maybe
no money and no dead things
A lot of buzzards
with not much to do
We would watch them for hours
sometimes instead of chopping cotton
stopping in the field
leaning on a hoe
lying by the big cedar.

Things Done Right

I

Now there are ruts in the floor
where Aunt Callie rocks with a morning cup of coffee
and warms her feet at a gas heater
whose black pipe shoots into the old chimney
where the fireplace had been.

But back when the ruts were young
the first sounds of morning were ashes being stirred
the thump of fresh logs
the pop of pine kindling in the cook stove
the quiet talk of the grownups
and the radio with its thin and fuzzy hillbilly music

> *How many biscuits can you eat*
> *this mornin' this mornin'*
> *How many biscuits can you eat*
> *this evenin ' this evenin '*
> *How many biscuits can you eat*
> *Pillsbury biscuits can't be beat*
> *this mornin' this evenin 'right now*

and the weather reports Uncle Vee always turned up.
We'd hear him walk to the door
and know he was looking at the sky

> *Don't care what the weather man says*
> *gonna rain this afternoon*

Then the radio would go down
and Aunt Callie and Uncle Vee would have their quiet time
and talk about the day
and he would say where he planned to work
and she would talk about washing or canning
or sewing or working the garden
and they would decide what we children would do
We'd hear the hiss of something frying
and wonder what it was before we could smell it

salt meat or bacon or maybe country ham

> *Better call those chirrun*
> *biscuits goin'in*

And the smells settling into the whole house
all the way under the covers
would help us wake up

II

Even in the hot of July
the cook stove was fired
and Aunt Callie baked biscuits every meal
using her big wooden dough bowl of flour
and pinching in lard and squeezing in buttermilk
working it only with her hands
then lifting the dough and rolling it out
cutting the biscuits with a baking powder can.

And there might be fried pies
sealed with a fork dipped in water
and pressed evenly along a crescent edge
Or a fruit pie with a tall crust
scalloped by the quick and perfect twists
of a buttered thumb and forefinger
Between meals Aunt Callie kept the stove hot
simmering a slow pot of string beans and salt meat
boiling water for dishes
heating irons on the day after wash day
How she would sweat in her loose wash dress
ironing everything from the clothesline
sprinkling with her hand dripping from a pan of water
sometimes pressing a cedar cutting under cloth
to make a pair of church trousers smell better
working fast before her iron cooled down
licking her finger and sizzling it against the iron
to check its hotness
as it sat on an old coffee can lid
at the end of the ironing board

And leaving no piece of cloth untouched
dish towels, sheets, tablecloths and wash rags
overalls and work shirts
which would be sweat wet and wrinkled in five minutes
even undershorts
and always making us boys change everything everyday

> *What if you's to be taken to the clinic*
> *or somethin'*
> *you want to be dirty?*

And folding everything on shelves and in drawers
as if they would never be touched
but be looked at and admired
and passed on
by some work clothes inspector.

On other days she churned
humming hymns to the wet rhythm of the dasher
the kitchen filled with bowls and buckets of milk
clabber or blue john or buttermilk
with cheesecloth keeping out the flies

III

And Uncle Vee was the same
the way he hitched his mule
and plowed his garden
geeing and hawing up and down the rows
always in the same direction
The way he put in his potatoes and onion sets
then unhitched the mule and fed and watered him
and always told the same stories

> *One time this old man asked his mule*
> *you want any more oats old boy*
> *and the mule lifted his tail*
> *and the sound came out his rear*
> *ffffeeewwwww*

and laughed and shook his head and slapped his knee
and said the punch line again

ffffeeewwwww

The way he measured two double handfuls of shorts
for each hog and mixed it with slop from the table
as if the hogs might not eat it done wrong
And in the evening after supper
laid a fire with pine knots and split wood
so it burned with one match
and never had to be stoked a second time
then sat with a cup of coffee
and always worked on something
maybe patching a stew pan with screws and a washer
or rigging a trotline or cleaning his double barrel
or sharpening his barlow knife
spitting on a whetrock
and drawing the blade toward him and away
and testing its sharpness against the hairs on his arm

> *Most dangerous thing in the world, boys*
> *is a dull knife*
> *cut you faster'n a sharp one*

and while Aunt Callie snapped peas or shelled butterbeans
he would peel an apple
putting his barlow to it and turning the apple
so the peel came in one long spiral
stretching halfway to the floor

> *You ain't peeled an apple*
> *till you can do that, boys*

And when we tried it
then and much, much later
the peel always broke and fell
and the apple never tasted the same

◆ ◆ ◆

Scenes of Courtship

I

They said she was an old crazy girl
who lived at the bottom of the hill
and we always honked when we went by
thinking of all the things we'd do with her
if only we had the nerve to stop

> *Blow the whistle Junior*
> *then step on it*

And we'd honk at any time of night
stepping on it before her father
could get to the window

> *He tole the sheriff*
> *he was gonna shoot anybody who honked*

On Saturdays when the crop was laid by
we'd put on khakis and a white shirt
hitched up two turns on the sleeve
our arms white above the sun browned hands
and we'd cock our elbows out the window
looking over our shoulders
sucking a match stick toothpick
and make the square slowly
but still spinning the tires on the turns
the white '46 Ford pickup washed with buckets from the creek
a white wall tire on the tailgate
and a skull turning knob on the steering wheel.
And we'd go to the dance at the national guard armory
and listen to Jimmy Deal and his Rythm Ranchers
and sip moonshine from fruit jars in paper sacks
and get brave enough to dance with country girls
because we thought they were easy
in their flour sack dresses
and their legs scratched from shaving with their daddy's razor

> *Now we gotta go straight home*
> *after the dance*

But we'd head for the moonlit cemetery
four in the pickup seat and always squeezing closer
when shadows moved among the stones

Start the motor
I know I saw somethin' that time

And our hands would fall in laps
and be pushed away
or our fingers would brush as if by accident
the soft bosom front of those flowered dresses
our khakis tightening with the intensity of that touch

I got my hand right on it Junior

II

But that was so much later
than when we courted at revival meetings
fanning through the singing and the preaching
every morning and every night
swimming in the afternoons
driving there in Winston's courting car
the '37 chevy truck with the cab cut off
open to the dust and gravel
taking a load to the creek and going back for more
jumping from the bank of the little Tobi Tubbi
named for an indian chief's wife
and the coldest creek in the country

Hey Winston dive on down
and bring us up some ice

And the girls would wear shorts over their bathing suits some
with the new elastic suits in light colors
and others in the old wool suits
that would get loose and sag open at the leg.
Someone would bring a watermelon from the creek
where it had been cooling
and we'd squirt the seeds from between our thumb and forefinger
until we were spotted
then jump in the Tobi Tubbi and wash them away

Y'all better come on
we gonna be late to revival

In the evening we wore
two toned cotton shirts starched
and we'd fan and sing and listen
and wait for the hayride to Mr. Bruce Wilford's melon patch

I bet you won't sit by Allie Jo
I bet you won 't kiss her

III

When the big boys went off to the war
and came home in their uniforms
we'd hide in the bushes where they parked
and watch them press their girls against the car seat
or sometimes in the summer
lean them backwards against the fender

> *He put his hand*
> *up her sweater Junior*

while we only played spin the bottle
at birthday parties
and didn't press against anyone
and didn't have uniforms

IV

It was a sin for a Baptist to dance
so we went with Methodist girls
who taught us to slow dance and jitterbug

> *Hey look at old Junior*
> *do the dirty boogie*

Then dance on the Tippah river bridge
to music from the radio
in Ben Edwin McKinsey's daddy's '39 Pontiac coupe

> *Now if this runs the battery down*
> *y'all got to help me push her off*

Until one time
when Betty Sue Wilford fell off the bridge
and broke her arm and got scratched up
and Ben Edwin had to carry her to Oxford in the coupe
and the old people found out about the dancing
and made us pray for forgiveness
and Ben Edwin couldn't get the coupe any more

V

But later when Junior bought the pickup from his daddy
and fixed it up
we had four in the front seat every Saturday night
and parked at the cemetery
and sometimes one couple would get back in the bed
on some hay and an old quilt Junior kept in a tool box
the girls always afraid the other was watching

>   *If they can see us*
>   *Marianne will tell everybody in school*

Until one night after a dance at the Water Valley armory
when I couldn't go
Junior and Betty Vee Fox hit ice on the Tallahatchee bridge
And all we could do was put black borders
around their pictures in the year book
where Junior was handsomest and Betty Vee was wittiest

VI

Then everybody graduated and got jobs
or went to the army
and there was a lot of marrying
And those who went to college
came back every once in a while
but didn't want country girls any more
and would not be seen in a pickup truck

◆ ◆ ◆

II. People, Places, Happenings

◆ ◆ ◆

Grave Digger

His name is Otis Cox
and the graves he digs with a spade are acts of love.
The red clay holds like concrete
still he makes it give up a place
for rich caskets and poor
working with sweat and sand
in the springing tightness of his hair
saying that machine digging
don't seem right if you know
the dead person.
His pauses are slow as the digging
a foot always on the shovel.
Shaking a sad and wet face
drying his sorrow with a dust orange white handkerchief
he delivers a eulogy

  Miz Ruth always gimme a dipper of water

Then among quail calls and blackeyed susans
Otis Cox shapes with grunt and sweat and shovel
a perfect work
a mystical place
a last connection with the living hand

◆ ◆ ◆

The Store

Up behind the store
doves roost in green kudzu
and black folks live in gray houses.
There we play in orange brown fields
between tall pines
quick as quail
running in black and white coveys
through boy high broom sedge.

Down in the summer dusty store yard
red mules suck green mossy water from wooden troughs
and men sit in caved cane chairs and suck wet peanuts from big orange drinks.
There we feel the mules' velvet gray noses
and pretend our light touch fingers are horseflies
tickling the long twitching ears.
Then scooping the vile water and flinging it at every close boy
we turn the dust to mud between our toes.

Inside the banana smelling store
men open Nehi belly washers and shake their heads about the weather
and women measure rat cheese and coal oil and softly pat new feed sack patterns.
There sitting on a floor shuffled thin by bare feet and brogans we catch slow
winged flies
and dash them into corner spiderwebs
watching their buzzing struggle until the quick step spider comes.
Then with tiny saving bites
we share a penny chocolate covered cream
its white and chocolate melting sticky
onto all our hands.

◆ ◆ ◆

Cousin Verdell on Food

When I eat those drumsticks from some chicken
who never scratched the dirt
I think of Cousin Verdell 's ideas about food

> *Best thing to eat*
> *is somethin' that'll eat*
> *somethin' else's droppin's*

And the thought of it made our mouths taste bad
and we figured Verdell was crazy

> *I tell you boys*
> *you think about it*

But we didn't want to
so we'd talk about fishing
and he'd talk about catfish

> *They eat dead stuff off the bottom*
> *I seen 'em eat manure*
> *and they absolutely the best tastin' fish*

Or we'd say we had to do chores
and he'd talk about pigs

> *Eat any damn thing*
> *eat they young'uns*
> *eat snakes*
> *eat all kinda slop*
> *and they absolutely the best meat*

There was no stopping him
until after the chickens

> *And chickens*
> *Boys they faller*
> *other animals 'round*
> *just to eat the corn outta they shit*
> *Hell they eat they own shit*
> *And what'd you rather eat than fried chicken?*

Verdell said God gave all those things a special organ
a purifying system
a way of taking what other creatures wasted
and turning it into something good.

But he wouldn't know what to say now
about a chicken who never scratched the dirt

◆ ◆ ◆

The Outhouse

I

It happens in places where they fold toilet paper
in little points
Where the seat is contoured
and the flush handle is from the modern museum
Where the tub is pastel
and the towels hang on heated bars
Where the sunlamps are on timers
and magnifying mirrors scissor out
to show the back of your head
That I think of all the terrors of the outhouse
on a dark and cold night
with wind bending the pines
with screech owls
with dogs howling in the bottom
and who knows what waiting
in that dark and putrid cavern below the splintery seat
maybe a new and unknown something
hatched from that awful murk
lying there or sliding or worming its way upward
waiting for that next soft bottom
to block its only view.
Or even things known and feared

> *One time an old boy over'n Union county*
> *got bit right on the dingus*
> *by a black widder. Died.*

II

We'd play so long and hard at the end of a day
we never wanted to stop

> *Now if you boys have to do a job*
> *you better do it before dark*

But sometimes we wouldn't
or we'd time it all wrong
or it would hit us after supper.
And how could the grownups tell?

> *You better go on out there now*
> *you can't wait till mornin'*

They always knew
and we couldn't undress for bed
until we took the coal oil lantern
and some pages from the catalog or newspaper
and after trying to get someone to come with us
just to stand outside
and after calling the dogs
who also seemed to know it was a wasted trip
whistled our way down the path
and into the shadowy drafty spidery three holer
talking loudly to no one
kicking the floor and seat
trying sometimes to squat balanced above the hole
so our bare skin would not be exposed to whatever there was
and finally
did our job (as Aunt Callie would say)
and made our way back
toward the lamp lit windows of the house

◆ ◆ ◆

Crow Killer

Why did he want to kill the crows
when he could talk to them
and call them up
and when they made him so happy
fighting owls and coming to his voice
when he created out of his own mouth
a battle
a mortal struggle
setting them against their old enemies?

But he killed them in a dozen clever ways
with a cow bell around his neck
and an old brown patchwork quilt over his back
crawling
on all fours among the cows
mocking their rhythm
swinging his head
ringing the bell
moving slowly toward the big beech tree
where the crows perched outsmarting everybody in the county
except Mr. C. W. the crow killer
who rose up from under the patchwork
with his double barrel
and got two
their awkward black bodies falling among the real cows
who hardly jumped when Mr. C.W. pulled the triggers.

But his favorite was the fight
the old owl crow fight
which started in his throat
and went out across the bottoms

      caw caw caw
      who-who
      who-whoo
      whoooooo
      whoooooo

Sending the message
that a bunch of crows had found an owl

had disturbed his daytime sleep
had set upon him
and were diving dodging driving
the old enemy from his resting place.
It was more than crows could resist
and they came to the sound
looking for the battle
eager to claim a piece of the kill
but Mr. C. W. was the killer
stepping from his hiding place
still cawing and hooting
right up until he pulled the triggers
always dropping two
black among the green leaves.

One time he almost missed
and a crow fell with a broken wing
and he took it home
and put it in his henhouse
with a splint on its wing
and fed it and trained it
to sit on his hand.
Then he took it to the woods and let it caw
while he hooted
a Judas crow
calling its friends and family
to die two at a time
one from each barrel.

One time I asked him why
and he said they eat corn in the field
and that seemed reason enough
but he fed his Judas crow corn from the crib
And when the crow died
old Mr. C.W. didn't come around much
but we would see him at the store
stocking up on shotgun shells
or hear him cawing and hooting
down in the woods
calling in crows
and killing them two at a time.

◆ ◆ ◆

Fox Hunt

Is it true the fox loves the hunt
and plays games with the pack
while men squat around fires
and boys stand back and slap mosquitos
or sleep on a car seat
or on the shelf of a coupe
or in a pickup
and wait for the chase?

>*Hike there! Speak to em!*
>*Speak to em!*

And do the dogs know they should not catch him
but just bark
and try to get ahead of the others

>*Old Peaches is moving up, Lester*
>*about in the middle*

and let their masters know
so they can talk about it
and spit in the fire and laugh at the sound
and teach the boys to love a dog's mouth
and know it as it comes out of the bottoms
through the pines?

>*Old Phoebe has kindly of a yodel,*
>*don't she*
>*a real pretty mouth*

And do the men think on the mystery of it
for boys bred hunters
to run to the crossing place
sucking the wet night air
pointing the flashlight and not a gun
for the shining of that red and white tail

>*Go to ground any time he wants to*
>*but he don't look tired yet*

Then light another fire and listen
as it settles on them
how foxes and other things
move easily through dark woods
leading their chase and going to ground
only at their pleasure?

The Copperhead According to Mother Ruth
(for her grandchildren)

Get him with a hoe
but don't step on the head
He'll bite you
even dead

Remember Aunt Callie
between heel and tree
he bit and ran
from Uncle Vee

Look in brushpiles
circle them wide
he's their color
and he'll hide

He's God's creature
but it's also true
you must do unto him
before he does unto you

◆ ◆ ◆

Christmas

I

We always talked about white Christmases
but there rarely was one.
They were mostly gray and wet cold
that cut through our mackinaws when we went for the tree
Preacher mule pulling the sled
down through the pasture and across a cotton field
with some unpicked still hanging ragged white on the stalks
to the bottom of cane and honeysuckle and sawbriars
and a few patches of cedars or pines.
We'd look at every tree

> *We could cut the top*
> *out of a big'un, Uncle Vee*

Then we'd tie it to the sled
and Preacher would pull it up the hill
his breath smoking from his nostrils
some of us running ahead
to tell the coming of the best Christmas tree

II

In the kitchen Allie Jo and Aunt Callie popped corn
from a little patch Uncle Vee planted every year
on the edge of a feed corn field
(and sometimes the August sun was so hot
it would pop on the cob)
and strung it on sewing thread
coiling it on the table
like a snake of popcorn
And we'd try a handful
complaining at the taste

> *We didn't put no salt on it*
> *'less you boys eat it all*
> *'fore we get it strung*

Uncle Vee mounted the tree on some scrap boards
and set it upright in a corner
across the room away from the fireplace

> *One spark boys*
> *and the whole house'd go*

When the popcorn snake was wrapped in and around the tree
we tied ribbons on the branches
and hung last year's Christmas cards
Aunt Callie had saved
most with a manger scene
or a picture of stained glass windows
(which we would see only years later
in city churches
where the people had money
and the preachers thought stained glass was important).
Sometimes we stuck cotton balls in the tree
and one year Aunt Callie tried making snow
from Ivory Snow like in a magazine
but it dried and crumbled on the floor
and Uncle Vee said it was more mess than it was worth.
We blew balloons and tied them like colored balls
and when the pine needles popped them
we would suck the rubber pieces
into little balloons in our mouths
then twist and tie them
making the tree shabby with colored rags of rubber

III

Cousin Hamer had a crystal radio with earphones
because he was blind from when one of his brothers
hit him in the eye with a sweetgum ball

> *Them boys was meaner'n house dogs*
> *but they didn't mean no harm*

and we took turns listening to Christmas carols
from big churches off somewhere

probably Memphis.
He would tune and tune the radio
and pass the earphones around
until the batteries got weak
and the music sounded farther and farther away
Then we'd sing for him
and have a prayer
and go home
always blowing out the lamps before we left
because he didn't need the light

IV

We got a few pieces of candy at Christmas
chocolate covered creams shaped like upside-down cones
and hard peppermints
and tangerines
like oranges that were easy to peel
Stockings
big boot socks full of tangerines
and pecans and jawbreakers and sometimes a grapefruit.
Uncle Vee always saved the biggest ham in the smokehouse
salt cured and smoked and two years hanging
and Aunt Callie would soak it and simmer it all day
then chill it in the coldest corner of the bedroom
farthest from the fireplace
and Uncle Vee would sharpen the butcher knife
until we'd be scared to touch it
and slice the ham so thin we could almost see through it

> *Mind grabbing those scraps like that boys*
> *good way to lose a finger*

We put the ham in biscuits
not fat dough biscuits but thin crusty ones
baked special for Christmas.
The rest of the food was the same as any Sunday
only there was more of it
maybe three kinds of meat
and more cakes and pies and teacakes
and we got to eat between meals

V

Morning was always early but Christmas was extra early
the first up stoking the fire and getting in wood
not complaining of the cold floor or the early chores.
Santa would have eaten his teacakes and drunk his coffee
and left us clothes mostly
a belt or gloves or rubber boots
or flowered shirts and dresses
from feed sack patterns we had seen in the feed shed
but never questioned that reindeer feed
must also come in printed sacks.
One year there was a mold for lead soldiers
and a little melting pot and a bar of lead

> *Now you got to be extra careful*
> *with that hot lead boys*

And we made the same soldiers
and killed them in battle
and melted them down
and made them again
until we burned out the mold

VI

Everybody acted happier
except when we prayed that all the soldier boys
would be home from the war by next Christmas.
We went to church and sang carols
and sometimes acted out the baby Jesus story
using old sheets and robes to be wise men and shepherds.
And the preacher said
wouldn't it be nice if we could keep
the spirit of Christmas all year long
And we thought it would be nice
and told ourselves we'd try

◆ ◆ ◆

Misplaced Woodsman

I see a woodsman in the parking lot
stopping amidst the cars
as if he did not have to stop
studying the stars
as if he did not know his direction now
smelling the air
as if seeking the wetness of a yonder river.

The woodsman's mind moves easily through the trees
barefoot across the slick bottom
bending poles and snapping sawbriars
leading the lost fishermen
out of the river
out of the storm.

I see a woodsman in the parking lot
turning at the car
as if waving the hunters ahead
bracing on the door
as if mounting a flat bed pickup
pressing and twisting
as if he needed no new legs.

The woodsman's mind cuts himself from under the fallen tree
hefting the McCullough with a sure hand
lifting limb by limb
making finally a crutch
complaining later that he should have stayed
until the job was done.

I see a woodsman in the parking lot
leaning as if there were no rubber tip cane
shading his eyes as if the pigeons
were a string of high geese
cupping his ear
as if expecting sudden wingbeats
or the bays of a far-off pack.

The woodsman s mind hears one voice among the hounds
figuring where the pack will cross
laughing at the red and white tail
sleeping later like the fox
the chase over
calmly gone to ground.

I see a woodsman in the parking lot
watching the sky for darkening clouds
as if no dams had stopped the floods
as if there were no beans where the water had been
measuring the horizon
as if the safe route were his to choose
as if no highways cut through the ancient hills
as if there were no air conditioned cab
no four wheel drive
no CB radio
As if there were none of those things to make life easy
without a woodsman.

◆ ◆ ◆

This photograph was taken in South Carolina in 1943; the men playing checkers were in Georgia 1939; and the sleeping dog, also in Georgia, escaped the sun in 1941; but the quiet spirit of a southern small town summer transcends time and place.
Photos: Library of Congress.

Mr. Sanford Hale, opposite page, was a hunter, farmer, husband, father, grandfather, friend, all those things which make a life. But perhaps he was proudest of his role in the Philadelphia Baptist church, near Oxford, Mississippi, where he was deacon and songleader. He and his singers traveled many a dusty road to all-day singings in the north Mississippi hills. In the top photograph, he was attending Philadelphia church s centennial. These photos are from a family album.

The church above was in North Carolina in 1939, but it could have been in a thousand different places, with its twin doors, one for each aisle, and its ubiquitous clusters of men on one side, talking farming, weather, and politics, and the women talking cooking, canning and children. Photo: Library of Congress

Left: A church benefit dinner in Kentucky in 1940. The ladies of the church baked for days then gathered to urge everyone else to eat.

Left and above, another dinner on the grounds in Kentucky, with the ladies peeling and slicing home-grown tomatoes. Under the trees the places are set, awaiting the singing, the praying, and the eating.
Photo: Library of Congress.

III. Flashbacks

◆ ◆ ◆

Progress

I

In the browning picture the whole town sits
man woman and child
smiling from the stump
workmen with axes and saws to the side.
How had it looked
a cypress big as a town's population
and tall as Poff Hill
its round top knees like children wading
all lamps and coffee tables now
and it confined as pecky paneling?

II

In the black dawn where the big trees had been
we waded mud for a mile
to the flat bottom boat
another mile on the water and we were not yet to the river
or beyond to the deep slash
of the duck, beaver, muskrat, egret, snake
their place gone now to beans
waist high across the bottomland
making forty bushels on an acre of memories

III

Boiling okra slimey stews and singing in Ira's pasture
cajuns channeled the Tippah and drained the old run
their big machines ripping the willows and straightening the bends
bringing land where the flood was
pushing out the cottonmouths and beaver dams
pushing out the bream the sweet willow catfish
pushing out the mysteries of the deep slash
proving it was mud and water after all

◆ ◆ ◆

Genealogy

You are
in these hills
who you were and who you will become
and not just who you are

> *She was a McKinstry*
> *and his mother was a Smith*

And the listeners nod
at what the combination will produce
those generations to come
of thievery or honesty
of heathens or Christians
of slovenly men or working

> *'Course her mother was a Sprayberry*

And the new name rises
to the shaking of heads
the tightening of lips
the widening of eyes

> *And his daddy's mother was a McIlhenney*

Oh god a McIlhenney
and silence prays for the unborn children
those little McKinstry Smith Sprayberry McIlhenneys

> *Her daddy was no count and her daddy's daddy was no count*

Old Brother Jim Goff said it
when Mary Allen was pregnant

> *Might's well send that chile*
> *to the penitentiary soons he's born*
> *gonna end up there anyway*

But that lineage could also forgive
with benign expectation
of transgressions to come

> *'Course, what do you expect*
> *his granddaddy was a Wilkins*

or

> *The Whitsells are a little crazy*
> *but they generally don't beat up nobody outside the family*

or

> *You can't expect much work out of a Latham*
> *but they won't steal from you*

In other times and other places
there are new families and new names

> *He's ex P&G*
> *out of Benton and Bowles*
> *and was brand management with Colgate*

And listeners sip Dewar's and soda or puff New True Lights
and know how people will do things
they are expected to do
New fathers spring up and new sons and grandsons
always in jeopardy of leaving the family

> *Watch young Dillard*
> *if he can work for Burton he's golden*
> *but he could be out tomorrow*

And new marriages are bartered for old-fashioned reasons

> *If you want a direct marketing guy*
> *get a headhunter after someone at Time Inc.*

Through it all
communities new and old watch and judge and make sure
the names are in order
and everyone understands

◆ ◆ ◆

Off Again
(Reflections of the Modern Traveler)

Off again
in all directions
like a chicken with his head cut off
like a blind dog in a meat packing house
like all those things
the old people would say
if they could see me now.

It was the same
plowing a mule geeing and hawing
in the hot wet sun
sweating a spot on the porch
at dinnertime
then off again
to the slanting red fields.

It was the same
hauling fertilizer to Memphis
stopping at the Toddle House
or the Villanova where a pork chop
cost more then a steak ought to
then off again
down the black top.

It was the same
on a Greyhound bus down '78
squeezing among the uniforms and hip flasks
walking the last ten miles
past the red schoolhouse and the soapstone gully
then off again
after the cotton was picked and to the gin.

Now it's all directions at once
with an air travel card
and a carry on bag
writing a speech working a budget
sweating a meeting chewing a Tums
like a chicken with his head cut off
like a blind dog in a meat packing house.

◆ ◆ ◆

Urban Flashback

Sitting somber in chauffeured cars,
surrounded by music and other people's stares,
wondering,
if I could go back
to laughing summer days
in '37 Chevrolet flat bed trucks
on dust-choking gravel roads.

Nodding with concern in padded conference rooms,
breathing cigar smoke and unscented deodorants,
wondering,
who here could recognize me
as I chopped at the threatening grass
and loosened the red sand soil
around the desperate cotton.

Smiling through dim rooms and light talk,
sipping something chic and soda,
wondering,
which of these ladies would bring
a covered dish and a quart of tea
to set among the prayers and songs
on the dinner grounds in the pine grove.

◆ ◆ ◆

Dialogue with the Past

What are you doing here
in this conference room
out of the cotton fields and red dust
looking over the coffee and pads
lined yellow and legal size
pretending to be a company man?
What do you expect me to think
with your country church and preacher man rightness
nodding at the plan
smiling at the chart
acting like the profit margins make a damn
when I know where you come from?
Who do you think you're kidding
the cowshit just off your shoes
not far enough from overalls
to be happy in a collar
with GQ in the briefcase
a charge at Saks
and your grandfather restless in the cemetery
every time the closet opens?

Wait wait
I'm the same and it is too
and nothing changes but the words
When the CEO shuffles his feet
in their Italian leather loafers
and calls for further study
and appoints a task force
it's one of the county supervisors
in overalls and brogans
kicking the dust and saying
well fellers sometimes I think, well
then again I just don't know
And everybody goes off and thinks about it some more

But what are you trying to prove
when you didn't have a pot to pee in
or a window to throw it out of
when the roof leaked and the rats came in
and you looking now to shelter
your money as well as yourself?

Only that I still want what I wanted
when you cut through the shit
to do to get to hang on to something
and I only made the trade
country church for conference room
deacons for directors
and chicken in the pot for a few shares of stock

◆ ◆ ◆

Smells of Life on Greyhound Buses
During World War II

There was a salty ham one time
a prize from the country
during meat rationing.

It covered the sweat
and sour smells
of summer wet undershirts
of field worn overalls
of overdue diapers.

After a while it filled the bus with thoughts of food
and talk of hot biscuits
and butter and red eye gravy

> You-ever-have-them-big-dough-biscuits
> you-could-stick-a-finger-in
> and-poke-a-place-to-fill with-butter-and-jeJly?

Suddenly
that ham made me center of the bus.
There was a staff sergeant
from Camp Currier, Missouri
and the old men called him sojer boy
and he became my friend
and patted the ham and said
he would cure his own again
when he got home from the war.

Sometimes now I wish for that salty smoky ham
but would it fit under the seats of 727s
on stratospheric routes
And could it work its aromatic magic
or would that man made unhuman air
blow it all away?

◆ ◆ ◆

Shades of Gray

Seeing the old gray houses along every back road
lose the fight with vines and weeds
I think of when the old place burned
and shotgun shells went off
as we watched from the big rocks
the fire too hot to get closer
and wondered what Uncle Vee would say
about the place he was born
and his preacher daddy died

> *Never shoulda rented it*
> *now it's gone*

But I think it was better for the old place to burn
full of stuff and not deserted
empty in the woods
good for a picnic pilgrimage and not much else
gray and bent like a crazy old woman
widowed and grandwidowed and great grandwidowed
until no one knows who she is
or how much she meant in those days
how she grunted out children on corn shuck mattresses
and nursed them and wiped them
all the time cooking and washing and hoeing
and weeding and gathering and canning
and waiting for the next baby
all of them gone and their babies gone
her eyes gray and vacant
looking through a screen door
in the old folks' home
still wearing a bonnet to a ragged garden
chopping grass with a hoe so many years sharpened it's now a sliver
living for those times when someone young comes
and surrounds her with life for a while
then goes again
leaving her wondering if there'll be a next time
her life fading grayer and grayer
like a house with vines and brush
with rusty roof and sagging porch
with snakes and rats and coons and birds
but none of the life that gave it a reason to be.

So I'm glad the old place burned when it did
still filled with life
still sheltering love and the coming of children

◆ ◆ ◆

IV. Worship

◆ ◆ ◆

Revival Meeting

How many heavy dusty nights
did I sit on wooden pews beside blonde sweating girls
stirring air toward them with funeral parlor fans
while infants slept finger sucking on quilts
and wasps flew heavy winged from lamp to lamp
searching for a place to fall and burn?

How many booming righteous promises of glory
did I ignore for whispered hints of ecstasy
while nervous deacons sun reddened in overalls
shouted self-conscious amens
and pale children pressed scared faces
into their mothers' laps?

How many stanzas of O Lamb of God I Come
did I sing on key and off
squirming with sweat sticking white shirt and khakis
still fanning and feeling that blonde warmth
while preachers pleaded voice catching phrases
and babies sucked late night breasts?

How many big and growing cousins
did I pat on work hardened backs
standing in the car fume night air
watching them twist hand rolled bull durhams into their lips
while bats swept wing dodging through the pole light
and blonde girls took sweat cooling walks?

How many veiled and wrinkled aunts
did I kiss on powdered cheeks
violet bath water smelling but sour
while blonde girls waited
on the pine needle ground beyond the tombstones
ready with slick and heavy tongue kisses?

And how many mornings have I sat
in the still warm and thick air of the empty church
reading the dim communion table carvings
while wasps not crisp dead like the others
flew in and out in and out
finding the lamps unlit and the sun too far away?

◆ ◆ ◆

All Day Singing with Dinner on the Grounds

I

There were old men with ear trumpets
who patted their feet against the rhythm
and sang notes melodious only to themselves
sitting near the front on an aisle
where some young cousin or nephew had led them.
Snuff staining the corners of their mouths
tobacco breath filling the rows around them
they stayed there most of the day
but the rest of us moved in and out
and new groups came
in cars and trucks and yellow school buses

> *Here come*
> *Mr. Sanford Hale*
> *and the Philadelphia singers*

Coming to the singing convention
coming from three or four counties away
on dusty roads over hills and through bottoms
in heat that made the radiators boil
and fresh ironed shirts go damp and wrinkled
in heat that made the britches stick to our legs
when we got up from the hard oak pews.
Coming to sing
in duets and trios and quartets
and some soloists like Miss Ernestine Lee
whose face had the light of God in it
when she sang How Great Thou Art

> *I declare*
> *you can hear Jesus*
> *in her voice*

And some congregation singing
different song leaders from different churches
taking turns

> Now we gonna ask
> Clyde Wyatt of Bethel Baptist
> to lead this next one

And sometimes they'd get up a quartet
from different churches
always discussing who would sing lead and who would sing bass

> *Now you come on up here Leon*
> *and you too Hamer*
> *and you sing alto Mr. J.W.*

And after two or three false starts
they'd sing all the old ones
all the ones everybody knew and heard on the radio
every Sunday morning before church
On the Jericho Road and
Take a Little Walk with Jesus and
My God is Real and
I Saw the Light

Sometimes they'd make all the ladies sing a verse
or all the children
or all the folks over sixty
Then between songs there'd be testimonials
or one of the preachers would lead a prayer
because all the preachers from all the churches came
and led a prayer before the day was over.

II

Late in the morning
by some signal I never saw
the ladies began to leave the church and go to the cars
and get baskets and sacks
and head to the dinnergrounds,
big gray tables under the trees
or sometimes rough lumber nailed between the trees,
and spread starched table cloths
and decide somehow among themselves
where the meat would be
and the vegetables and bread
where to gather the cakes and pies
and jugs of iced tea.
Then someone would let the songleader know
and he'd say that dinner was ready
and everybody would go outside and have another song
and a prayer
then start along the tables
smiling at their neighbors

thanking God for the day
spooning their plates full

> *Now you boys just keep back*
> *and let them ladies go first*

It seemed all the food in the world
fried chicken crisp and soggy
country ham and sausage in biscuits
deviled eggs and creamed corn
and blackeyed peas and okra
and green beans and sliced tomatoes
and corn bread and spoon bread
and all manner of pies and cakes
stacked apple pies and Mississippi mud pies
pound cakes sliced thick with strawberries and cream
big wet banana cakes
and coconut cakes you ate with a spoon.
And the ladies would watch to see
whose dishes got eaten first

> *Miss Nora*
> *you just can't make enough*
> *of them old time buttermilk pies*

and smile and say how this wasn't near as good
as they usually make.

III

Then the singing would start again
with people coming and going
with men and boys standing outside the open windows
rolling cigarettes from little sacks of tobacco
picking their teeth with black gum brushes
and spitting into the red powder dust.
And later in the afternoon
we'd go off into the pines behind the church
and throw rocks
and shoot green plums from our slingshots
and not really listen to the singing any more
but hear it anyway
and the motors starting
and the people getting on the schoolbuses
and our names called when it was time to go.

◆ ◆ ◆

Baptism

He waded into the cold water up to his knees
then across a sandbar and into the current
and turned and called to us
and suddenly the swimming hole was different.
We'd been there for a thousand swims
but it was different
colder maybe
swifter
deeper
surrounded not by boys and girls in swim suits
but by Sunday dressed ladies and coat and tied men
singing

> Shall we gather at the river
> the beautiful the beautiful
> river

And we moved in a line
barefoot and in white shirts and wash pants
the girls in dark colored dresses
which would not show through when they got wet
Across the shallows onto the sandbar
and from there went one at a time
in the name of the father, the son, and the holy ghost
to be put under the water
his arm behind our shoulders
and his hand over our mouth and nose
and our hand on his hand
For only a few seconds but it seemed longer
longer than any time when we had jumped or dropped from a vine
longer than when we swam underwater to scare the girls
longer than we thought we could ever stand
but he pulled us up
and said amen and the people said hallelujah
and our mothers hugged us as we went wet onto the bank.

Then he came out of the water
and we sang On Jordan's Stormy Banks I Stand
and he lifted his arms over us
all shivering there
the water draining from our pants cuffs
dresses clinging to the girls' legs

And said some words
about our sins washed away
and cleansed in the blood
and born again
And told us we were saved
and would go to heaven
and have life everlasting
and many other important things
we remembered for a long time.

◆ ◆ ◆

V. Death

◆ ◆ ◆

Photo: Library of Congress

Death in the Family

I

People hug us and cry
and pray we'll be strong
and know we'll see her again someday
And we nod and they pat and rub
reassuring her to heaven

> *She's with Jesus now*
> *no suffering where she is*

Then sit on hard benches and sing
of precious memories how they linger
and farther along we'll understand it

> *Cheer up my brother*
> *We're not forgotten*

The preacher studies his Bible and stares at the ceiling
and the song leader in his blue funeral suit sweats
and strokes the air
with a callused hand

> *We'll understand it*
> *all bye and bye*

And powdered and rosy cheeked
Miss Anne sleeps in an open coffin
the children standing tiptoe to see through the flowers
but scared to go near and drawing back when lifted
And the choir brings a balm in Gilead
and a roll is called up yonder

> *When the trumpet of the lord shall sound*
> *and time shall be no more*

And big men shake heads white at the hat line
while women weep and flutter air with palm leaf fans
And later we stand amidst the stones
by the mound of red clay
our eyes wet against the sun

and listen to preachers and mockingbirds
and the 23rd Psalm

II

Men stand uneasy in ties
and nod their hats to ladies
and kick gravel with shoes too tight
and talk about life

> *Nobody no better'n Miss Anne*
> *No Sir*
> *No Sir*

Smoking bull durhams around the porch
shaking their heads to agree
and sucking wind through their teeth

> *Never let you go thirsty*
> *bring a jugga tea to the field*
> *ever day*

They open doors for us and look at the ground
as if by not seeing our faces they become invisible
There are not enough chores
so three draw well water
and two get the mail
and four feed the dogs
and the rest chop wood
and wish for something to say

> *Lester broke his arm one time*
> *and Miss Anne plowed that mule*
> *like a man*
> *put in the whole crop*

And they talk of crops and plowing
of rain and sun and flood and drought
The seasons passing in memory
marking changes in years and lives
that men remember at times
when there's nothing to say

III

Ladies come with sad faces
and baskets of sweets
teacakes, pecan pies, puddings, memories
and we choose and they serve
telling stories and god blessing the children

>   *I declare that Miss Anne*
>   *was the sweetest Christian person*
>   *in the world*

Saying all the things to be said
doing all the things to be done
like orderly spirits
freshening beds from the grieving night
poking up fires gone cold
filling the table and sideboard
then gathering there to urge and cajole
as if the dead rest easier on our full stomachs

>   *Lord how Miss Anne would have loved that country ham*

No sadness so great it cannot be fed away
by the insistent spirits

>   *That banana cake is her very own recipe*
>   *I remember how she loved my spoon bread*
>   *She canned the berries in this cobbler*

And suddenly we are transformed
and eat and smile and thank you
and the ladies nod and know they have done well again
in time of need
And the little girls watch and learn
And we forget the early spring cemetery
and the church with precious memories
and farther along we do understand it
the payments and repayments
of all the ladies that were and are
and we pray ever will be. Amen

◆ ◆ ◆

Prayer for a Country Preacher

Oh God
let him go dreaming when he goes
let him go preaching a revival meeting
with the congregation eager beyond discomfort
on a wet and insect laden night

let him go singing bass
on a Sunday morning
his head above the others
his voice bringing power beyond
power in the blood

let him go walking the river bottom
leading the lost fishermen through the storm
breaking saplings to mark the trail

let him go wading the shallows
his boots sucking mud in the dawn
calling the green headed mallard
shooting quick and sure

    Not bad for a country preacher

let him go praying
at a table of summer Sunday food
fried chicken and sliced tomatoes
and peas and cornbread and tea
with his family around him
like disciples

Oh God if he must go
let him go dreaming

◆ ◆ ◆

Death Message

How long have I waited
for this late night phone ringing?
To come awake knowing
and to lie awake thinking
And it came on a night
when I heard a far-off train
calling in two tones
letting everyone know it was
moving on down the line.

Far-off trains and dying people
roll together through my life
as if no one in Mississippi
can die without a mourning train
to start the dogs howling
to set loose all the sounds
of a world turned sad.

In that night and dawning
unreal rafters reveal themselves
above the bed
a thin memory of rough sawn boards
and dawns under a tin roof.
Then a jet whines
no mourning train but a space machine
returning me to a lifetime ago.

◆ ◆ ◆

Against All Those Desperate Prayers

Against all those desperate prayers
whispered in airplanes
and hospital corridors
Against all those deals and bargains
of new beginnings and new behaviors I thought God
could not afford to pass up
Against all the wild promises
he died anyway.

◆ ◆ ◆

Life After Mississippi

Photography by Lola Mae Autry

to Sally...
    ...for whom I am thankful every single day

CONTENTS

◆ ◆ ◆

ACKNOWLEDGMENTS AND THANKS

Knowing where to begin is the hard part of writing acknowledgments. So many people played some part in this book or in my life, or both, that I cannot possibly name them all. Nor would naming them pay the proper tribute for all they have done.

Rather than apologize further for what I can't do, however, let me do what I can.

First, I thank my wife, friend, and critic, Sally, to whom this book is dedicated.

Next, I thank my sons: Jim, who in resisting all the pressures of the past 18 months, has taught me much about courage; Rick, who in living his life as if he had no handicap at all, has taught me much about the much-maligned power of optimism; and Ronald, who in his five blessed years of life, has taught me much about patience and trying to live in the grace of each moment. All three sons are woven throughout several poems in this book.

I thank my stepmother, Lola Mae Autry, for her wonderful photographs. What started as a way to illustrate my father's articles has become an almost full-time profession for her. It should be said that many of these photos have required her best darkroom skills in restoration and printing of some very old "box-camera" snapshots. These pictures are not intended as specific illustrations for the poems; rather they are their own expression of a time and place.

And I thank my Mississippi family, brother Lanny and sister Martha Lynn and their families, Deborah and Susan and Amy, and Ray and Clint.

My cousin Douglas has been a constant friend and inspiration to me for many years. His wife, Elizabeth, is among the most abiding and supportive people on earth. They have consistently nurtured me with their generous spirits.

And I must acknowledge the people of the Abel's Store community and Pine Grove Church. They and their kin appear throughout my poetry, but as I tell them when I visit: "Don't try to figure out who's who in these poems; I've moved the facts around, and only the truth remains."

Also a part of this book and of my life are my sister-in-law Susie, widow of my brother, and her children, Susan and John, and their families.

And I thank my publishers, Larry and Dean Wells, who took the leap in publishing my first book in 1983. I thank them for their confidence, and I thank them for continuing to run a high-quality regional press in the face of today's business pressures.

Finally, I thank you, the readers who responded so enthusiastically to "Nights Under a Tin Roof." It was your support that led directly to the publishing of this book.

J.A.A.
Des Moines, Iowa
May 4, 1989

INTRODUCTION
by Willie Morris

Jim Autry and I have many things in common. We both grew up in Mississippi then went away from it to work in the magazine trade, to write and to edit other people's writings. What we share most strongly, however, is a regard for our native ground, for the people and traditions there.

Jim was raised in the hill country of North Mississippi, in Benton County. I consider myself a flatlander, having grown up in Yazoo City, where the hills meet the delta. My people always sympathized with the folks "up north in those hills" who had to wrench a living out of hard ground. Yet we had an inordinate respect for the hill people's endurance and strength, their tenacious religion and friendships and family ties that seemed as tough as the rocky land that spawned them.

These are the qualities that I sense in my friend, Jim Autry, both the man and the poet. In his distinguished verse he shares with us the power of his faith in mankind, his sense of community in the face of adversity. He takes us back and forth between the past and present, between the youth that we remember and the future we face together. His poems reflect the lessons life teaches: "Grabblin' " is about rites of passage, about where courage comes from; "Flavors" reminds us of youth and innocence and the simple joy of being; "Fishing Day" takes us back in a rush to the great Mississippi outdoors; "Ordination" is about change, about new beginnings.

Life After Mississippi is Autry's tribute to his Mississippi roots, to the places and people that nurtured him and which now sustain him in the corporate boardrooms of America, in anonymous, scented hotel rooms, on 747 flights from New York to L.A. while he sits strapped in his seat writing about half forgotten funerals in country churchyards. As a successful executive he keeps his mind on his work but his heart, as they say, is down home.

> *Yet it is with me still*
> *in the fall smell of wood smoke*
> *from some suburban chimney*
> *in an Atlanta taxi driver's turn of phrase,*
> *in the quiet of an old church in Bavaria...*

For what Autry is writing about, again and again, is home. He listens to voices heard and unheard, and he touches something deep in our hearts. He is an observer whose task it is to remind us of those small but important details that add up to a significant understanding.

"Life," he writes, "is largely a matter of paying attention."

I. Mississippi

◆ ◆ ◆

Fishing Day

I

Old ladies in bonnets fished
with cane poles,
baiting their hooks with worms
or grubs from under a wet log
turned over by one of us boys.
They sat,
long sleeved against the mosquitos
and watched cork bobbers
and caught small bream,

> *Lord, they are the sweetest little fish.*
> *Fry 'em crispy and eat 'em*
> *bones and all*

tossing them in a bucket
where they splashed and swam a while
then turned belly up,
their gills moving in and out
slowly until they died.

II

We would go to the bottom early,
in a mule wagon,
men and boys and women and girls
and babies and dogs and all,
and the men and boys would find
a flat dry place
and start fires and cut green brush,

> *Build up a little smoke, boys,*
> *keep them skeeters away*

and the women and girls would spread quilts
and sometimes make a mosquito net tent
for the babies
but most times would just fan them,
or we'd build shelters of branches
if it looked like a sprinkle,
and always a big cooking fire.
We brought flour sacks and tow sacks
full of iron skillets
and salt and corn meal and lard.
We brought plates and knives and forks and glasses.
There were gallon jugs of tea
and always cakes and pies.

III

But we couldn't eat until we caught fish,
not little bream but catfish,
blues and willows and yellows and channels,
on set hooks.
First some of us cut saplings or cane
then trimmed and sharpened the ends
while others seined for bait
in the little sloughs and backwaters
left from when the river flooded.

> *You boys watch for cottonmouths,*
> *they like them sloughs.*

Then we'd unroll our hooks
one at a time,
big claw hooks on heavy cotton cord
with nuts and washers and whatever else
for weight,
and tie them to the poles.
Under a low-hanging tree was good
or the downstream side of a log
or around a drift,

> *Mind you don't set so close in there,*
> *he'll hang you on a branch and slip away*

jamming the sharpened end of the pole
deep into the mud bank,

> *Stick it deep, boys.*
> *I lost a pole one time that was a foot*
> *in the bank. Pulled it out and swam off.*

then pushing the pole down parallel to the water
until the hook touched bottom
and the line bowed,
then up just a few inches.

> *Come and get it, Mr. Catfish.*

IV

When we had set maybe a hundred hooks
we seined more bait,
then we ran the hooks,
moving along the slick bank,
checking each hook, rebaiting,
always hoping the next pole
would be jerking,
slapping the water,
then arguing over whose turn it was
to land the fish.

V

The women who did not fish sat on quilts
and fanned with palm leaf
or funeral parlor fans
and talked about the heat
or the mosquitos or something they heard at church.
And they yelled at the children
to stay back from the bank.

> *You slide in that water*
> *we'll never see you again.*

And sometimes one might sing a church song
while the others listened or hummed,
and one might do some sewing,

> *I swear, Nora, you make*
> *the straightest little stitches.*

and they would watch
how the fishing was going
and tend the cooking fire
until the coals were right.

VI

The men never wanted to eat
because they came to fish
but the little children would get fussy
and the women would spread a place,

> *Boys, better clean some of them fish*

and we would punch a hole
at the back of the catfish's head
and run a broom straw down his backbone,

> *Paralyzes 'em.*

then cut the skin enough to grab it with pliers
and pull it right down to his tail,
first breaking his fins at the base.

> *Git them fins before they git you.*

With a big one,
at least ten pounds,
we'd nail him to a tree,
through the head,
then make the cut and skin him.
The guts were a mess
but we kept some parts for bait,

the only fun of it
seeing what was in his stomach.
You'd be surprised what we found sometimes,
a whole turtle, shell and all,
a little snake,
one time a mouse,
and the girls hated it.

VII

The women would roll catfish steaks
in corn meal
then put them in a skillet of hot lard,
with sliced potatoes in another,
and hushpuppies after the fish,
and the girls would get out the slaw and tea.

>   *Boys run git the men*
>   *and tell 'em we're ready*
>   *for the blessing.*

And we would bow our heads
while a deacon gave thanks
for the day and the fish
and the fellowship,
and blessed the food to the good
of our bodies, amen.

VIII

In the afternoon there were naps
and more fishing
and quiet talking
and sometimes a rain shower
which nobody minded
and which usually made the fish bite better,

>   *Look at 'em. They're loading on.*

all of us wondering why that was.
Then we'd begin to load the wagon,
the men arguing about
whether to take up the lines
or bait them overnight
and come back in the morning.
We always left the hooks
because no one could resist the possibility
of coming tomorrow and finding
a pole bent into the water
straining against the biggest catfish
we would ever see.

◆ ◆ ◆

Mister Mac

People didn't know how to take Mister Mac,
"whippoorwill" they called him
because his nose made him look like one,
and laughed when he ran,
the only Republican in the county.

     Feel we need a two-party system.

Still, something was sad about his twenty or so votes,
though he said it was more
than he had family;

     Musta convinced a few.

and went on about his business,
writing insurance
for companies who wished
they could get someone else,
but nobody in the territory
wanted to bump Mister Mac
out of the job,
his being the only support for his sisters,
and most of the people having gone to school to him
at one time or another,
back when he was one of the few educated men
in the area,
though even then they didn't know whether to admire
or feel sorry for him
because it was not easy to be educated
and amount to much in those days.
So they called him whippoorwill
and dodged his car
when he drove, cataracts and all,
to the square,
where he would soften them up
with humor,

     You never been choked
     till you been choked on a sweet tater.

then tell all who would listen
how the South would never rise again
without a two-party system,
ending with his favorite story.

One time the judge asked this man,
"Henry, what you got to say
before I sentence you to hang
by the neck till dead?"
Henry said, "Judge, I just
want to say it sure is gonna
be a lesson to me."

But "peculiar" was the word they used,
not eccentric, like nowadays;
"kinda peculiar," they'd say.
Mister Mac thought they admired his spunk
despite how they treated him,

      Trying their best not to listen,
      they hear me though.

but when he died and his cousin sobbed
all through the service
and told me, "Jimmy there's not a dry eye
in this town today,"
the preacher had to ask the people
to bunch up in the front
so it would look like a crowd.

◆ ◆ ◆

Cousin El

When I remember my childhood Mississippi
I think of Cousin El
who lost his sight to a sweet gum ball
and lived the rest of life on the home place.
Did he always see those hills and fields and trees
as they were when he was a child
throwing sweet gum balls with his brothers?
And will I always see that place
as it was,
sweet and green and dusty,
and not as it is now,
a kind of blindness protecting me
from the video stores and pizza shops
and straightened rivers
and thinned forests?

The answers are yes and yes,
but here's the difference:
I indulge the blindness,
and Cousin El would have loved to see the changes,
ugliness and all.

◆ ◆ ◆

Grabblin'

The word is grappling
but we said grabblin'
and bragged that Mississippi
was the only state with a season for it,
our real boast being that Mississippi
was the only state
with men and boys brave enough to do it,
to crouch in the water
and reach up under the bank,
bare-handed,
searching a slick hole
hoping for a catfish
and not a snake or snapper or dogfish
or any of the dangers
we knew could be under those waters.

II

We went in big groups,

> Don't ever grabble by yourself, boys,
> a 15-pound catfish can drown you.
> He's got you much as you got him.

six or eight men and that many boys,
in overalls and barefoot
or wearing our most wore-out shoes,
starting miles up the river
and wading the shallows,
which was most of it,
dropping into holes here and there,
waist or shoulder deep,
to poke around sunken logs or drifts
or under the mud banks.

III

Every boy had to catch a catfish,
sticking a thumb in the sandpaper mouth
and fingers in the gills,
pulling him from his den
where the precious eggs lay.

Be sure you got those gills
or he'll spin on your thumb
and peel the skin like a onion.

We'd put our catch in big tow sacks
dragging them behind us in the water
and when we rested we'd open the sacks
and tell our stories

That there jughead
got a piece of my thumb.

remembering each fish and its part of the river.
Grabblin' was for big fish
and we caught twenty- and thirty-pounders,
sometimes two men wrestling one
onto the bank
then resting out of breath
at the work of it.

IV

There may have been a thousand snakebites
and there may have been none;
though we boys expected snakes in every hole
our fear of shame was stronger than our fear of snakes.

Stick your hand on in there, boys,
a snake'll run from you,
you couldn't touch one if you tried.

We saw so many on the bank
and dropping from tree limbs as we moved toward them
that we held our breath
every time we reached into a hole
or we pretended to talk to the fish
the way the men did

Okay, Mr. Catfish, I need me something
to make the gravy stink tonight.

V

Sometimes a grabblin' would end
with a fish fry or big stew;
the women and girls gathering with all the food,
except fish,

in Ira's pasture where we would wade
out of the river
and dump our sacks onto the grass.
Then we'd clean fish
and change clothes
and show our blooded thumbs
to the little boys
and the girls,
telling them yes we saw snakes
but you can't worry about stuff like that
if you want to be a grabbler.

◆ ◆ ◆

When Boys Wanted To Go To War

When I sneaked the flashlight under the covers
and read comics
until the precious batteries were weak,
I learned all how to hate my enemies.

First
on those pages
with the shadow pictures of babies on bayonets
with their mothers looking terrified
while demonic Nazis and Japs
prepared to stick their gleaming daggers
you know where,
with the Nazi pilots
shouting, "Die you swine,"
as they machine-gunnned our pilots
parachuting from their burning
Lightnings or Mustangs or Spitfires.

Then
in church where
someone's son or brother was dead
and there was no turning the other cheek.

And
in a dozen hot red dust cemeteries
with honor guards and seven-gun salutes
making the babies wake and cry,
where there were little brothers itching
to grab those honor guard rifles
and load them with real bullets
and go get those dirty murderers.

And some little brothers did go
and some were too young
but went to Boy Scouts
and did close order drill like the army,
and hoped the war would last a long time.

❖ ❖ ❖

II. Leaving
Mississippi

◆ ◆ ◆

Leaving Mississippi

Part of me never left
and another part is always leaving,
leaving Mississippi but never gone.
"Jimmy when you gonna come on back
down home?" my people ask,
and I cannot say, "Never,
I've found my home somewhere else"
any more than I can say my home
was never in the State of Mississippi
but in the community of it,
in my father's churches,
in Abel's store,
in Ashland on the square,
in how the people were together.
Now that home is gone forever from Mississippi -
yet it is with me still,
in the fall smell of wood smoke
from some suburban chimney,
in an Atlanta taxi driver's turn of phrase,
in the quiet of an old church in Bavaria,
in the call of an Iowa night hawk,
in a fish breaking the surface of a Colorado stream,
in the night peepers everywhere
in a stanza of Amazing Grace,
in the crickets,
in dust.

◆ ◆ ◆

Saying Goodbye

Every time I say goodbye to the old folks
I know it may be the last time,
and when it turns out to be,
I am still surprised
and regret the things I did not say,
so now I machine-gun the news to them,
everything I said at the past goodbye
and will say at the next one,
as if loading them with stories
and recollections
to take along
if they go before I return.

Yet I know I still will regret
the things I did not say,
the words that would cloud us up
and make us look at our shoes
and cause one of them to say,
"Aw save that talk till they're ready
to put me in the ground."

So I keep those words to myself,
not wanting anyone to think
I see death coming.

◆ ◆ ◆

"Your Uncle Vee Had A Massive Stroke Last Night"
June 23, 1987

Poem 1.

I always throw the number away
as if I'll never need it again,
then comes a call
and I dial the old 601-555-1212
and ask for Tippah County Hospital,
hearing those seven digits I've heard so often,
then punching the buttons,
dreading the voices,
dreading the things that won't be said.

Poem2.

Uncle Vee is the last one now,
and I wonder if he's the only man in Mississippi
who still lives in a house he built
of raw lumber sixty years ago,
who plowed a mule in red clay,
over and around hills,
not a flat spot on the place,
who cursed crows in the garden
and hawks and foxes and chicken snakes,
who killed hogs and cured meat and smoked it,
who ate pork and greens and cornbread,
and drank gallons of buttermilk,
and got bigger and bigger
but at eighty-six was still hungry every day,
who taught six grades in the same red schoolhouse
before it was blown to bits by the Second Army
on maneuvers in Holly Springs National Forest,
who taught singing school
and led the choir
and took busloads of singers
to singing conventions all around five counties,
who served in the legislature
where he wore a tie every day,
and who was cheated out of the election
by a kind of politics he thought was a sin.

Poem 3.

Now Uncle Vee wants to go home,
he wants to sing hymns,
he wants to feel a plow breaking the ground,
he wants to drive his old car to the store
and talk about the weather
and buy somebody a belly washer
and smell the hoop cheese and coal oil.
He wants to see his wife
ironing in her straight wash dress,
wiping sweat with the back of her hand.
He wants to smell her biscuits
and put a dipper in the sweet water
she brings from the cistern.
He wants to hear his children
playing around the porch.
So he tries,
he wakes and pulls at the tubes
when the nurses aren't looking,
and cries when finally I reach him
on the telephone.

◆ ◆ ◆

Mortality

It's my turn to become my father,
liver spots, knotty hands and all,
time for me to tell my stories so many times
that someone thinks he should tape-record them
for his grandchildren
who will never know me.
Verdell is already his father
and I have heard his stories
of Calhoun and Leroy and Jimmie Lee
and I have turned on the tape recorder,
a sure sign.

◆ ◆ ◆

Flavors

It happened again
this time with blackberry jelly and bacon,
together like a cold morning
in Mississippi,
the fire popping and someone stamping his feet,
and troves of warmth here and there,
in front of the fireplace, around the kitchen stove,
from a bed with the covers thrown back.

It happened this time in one of those places
with toasted white bread
and grilled bacon cured with a needle
instead of in a smokehouse,
and Knott's Berry Farm blackberry preserves
from a one-serving jar,
even an orchid on the table.

Yet I could squint at those far from home palm trees,
and despite the china and crystal,
my pressed cuffs, dry-blown hair and Old-Spice smell,
could squeeze the blackberry and bacon
between my tongue and the roof of my mouth,
tasting and tasting,
all the old flavors again.

◆ ◆ ◆

Ordination

for the Rev. Ms. Patricia Ryan

Brother Jim Thompson came,
the oldest,
with overalls and a white shirt buttoned at the collar,
with a walking cane and a Bible
that had stood fifty years of pounding,
and with that old fire burning through his cataracts.

> *Didn't need no seminary.*
> *Always preached the Bible*
> *and the Lord Jesus Christ*
> *crucified and buried and*
> *raised from the dead.*

Brother Hamer came
and Brother Ewart
and the three Walker boys,
preachers all.
They came through rain,
wrestling the wheels of their out-of-county cars,
sliding in ruts so deep the tail pipes dragged.
They parked under the trees
and along the road,
then walked, shined shoes and all
through the mud,
picking their way along the high spots
like children jumping puddles.
Into the church of their fathers,
the place they had all felt the call,
the old home church
where thousands of hands had pressed
on the bowed heads of new preacher boys,
of sun-reddened young men called by the Lord,
called from the cotton fields to preach the word.
They had felt the hands,
these old preachers,
felt those blunt-fingered, work-hardened hands,
felt them like a blessing,
like an offering, like a burden.
Felt them at weddings and baptizings,
felt them in the heat of a summer revival sermon,

in the agony of a baby's funeral,
in the desperate prayer against some killer disease,
in the frustrating visit with a mind gone senile.
And now the old preachers come to lay their hands
on the head of a new kind of preacher,
a preacher from the seminary,
a preacher who studied the Bible in Greek and Hebrew,
who knew about religions they never heard of,
who knew about computers
and memory banks full of sermons
and many other modem things.
A new kind of preacher,
and yet,
a preacher who still would feel on her head
the hands
like a commandment
from all the preachers and deacons who ever were.

◆ ◆ ◆

Goodbye Truck Stop Girls

I

There was one not far from New Albany
named Velma
who could do the dirty boogie on one foot
all the way to the floor and up again
if you would feed the jukebox and her pocket.

And there were others
named Mavis and Erlene and Wilma
and Inez and Bettyanne
and Lottie Sue and Sarah Vee
and they could all boogie and jitterbug
and wait tables at the same time
and take care of themselves
no matter what anybody said.

And the ones who didn't marry some old boy
and have babies
to bring back and show off
to the cooks and cashiers and other girls
got older and meaner
and started using coarse words
when we would feed the juke
and warned the younger girls about us
and then went on to do whatever they do
always in another town.

II

But something happened:
the juke music changed
and good old boys became cowboys
and the truck stop girls put on tight jeans
and cowboy boots
and talked about snorting toot
and asked the truck cowboys for bennies
and yellowjackets and stuff we never heard of

and broke out in a bunch of names
like Debbie and Lynn and Tammie
and Dawn and Renae
and Tanya and Crystal
and squealed into CB radios
for cowboys to stop in
and would hardly wait on anybody
and would never dance to the juke
no matter how many quarters we pumped.

◆ ◆ ◆

Television And The Church

Every time I find myself in the little church
where my grandfather and father
preached,
where my uncle led singing conventions
while someone played an upright piano
and pumped an old organ;
every time I feel the air-conditioning
and hear the latest hit
from the Top Forty Christian Countdown,
I think,
Damn you, television.

◆ ◆ ◆

Mississippi Writers Day

The irony was lost on no one.
There we sat,
poets, writers, teachers, scholars,
in the chamber where some
of our grandfathers and great-grandfathers
deliberated on how to solve
the nigra problem,
then passed the poll tax
and set up separate but equal schools
and decided that everyone had to read
and understand the constitution
before he could vote.
We sat there,
in the chamber in the building
whose bricks were made by slaves.
We sat and listened
to black poets,
to angry black poets
who read their words
so that no one could ever feel safe
reading them in a white voice.

It was a lesson about words
and how their color changes.
It was a lesson about places
and how their power changes.
It was a lesson about people
and how their fear changes.

◆ ◆ ◆

Elegy For A Gentle Person

She was sitting on the porch
in a cane bottom chair
leaning against the wall by the front door
watching them shoot blanks at the red schoolhouse
and throw smoke bombs through its windows,
her daddy shaking his head and cursing,

> *Reckon we'll win this war*
> *if the Japs hole up in a schoolhouse*

when the soldier came around the cistern
and stole her heart
just like in the stories.
Later, some said he was ignorant and worthless,
a lazy no count,
and she was the only one surprised
when he left after the children were born.
But back then he was handsome
in the uniform
and even her daddy saw new possibilities.

Everyone said God knows she tried
but what could you expect
from a man with no class at all,
and some worried about how the children
would turn out
but she was from a good family
and was a hard-working mother.
Money was scarce and after a while
so were her healthy days,
heart trouble, they said,
and long times not able to work.
But she did not complain
even when the children grew up and moved out,
and if she ever thought about her soldier
she did not say.

Some said her life was small
and she must have been lonely
and how could she have kept going,
but she did not ask these questions,

busy as she was
going to church when she felt up to it,
watching the TV,
helping her mother and daddy in their age,
sitting sometimes on that same porch
across the road from where
the schoolhouse had been -
now a flat spot so barren
that no one could ever imagine
there had been children
and games
and laughter
and bells.

◆ ◆ ◆

Funeral For A Gentle Person

Behind the coffin,
flowing from the pews,
brother, sister, children, grandchildren, cousins, aunts,
a river of kinship bears her
to a place we hope she dreamed about,
all those days alone
in a small house
by the side of a busy road,
no cars stopping.

◆ ◆ ◆

Life After Mississippi

I

The question always hanging
behind my head is
"Can I make it to Mississippi?"
Every old car I've looked at and bought,
"Will this baby make it to Mississippi?"
Every tank of gas
will almost get me back to Mississippi.
Every paycheck has to be enough
at least for a bus ticket
even though I don't want to go.
Long ago I could have stopped worrying,
but now it could be war
or the great depression
or cancer
sending me back into the family land,
where I'd walk through a woodsy bottom,
a world as far away as it used to be,
and I would garden and hunt
and fish clean streams,
and eat catfish and bream with no spots in their flesh,
and store onions and potatoes in a root cellar,
and be a neighbor to everyone
for as long as we lasted.

II

I know a crease between the hills
where water comes from under a rock.
A little digging
and I'd have a spring
where I would take my bucket to fill every day
and leave a gourd so others could drink.

III

Sooner or later
the snake would come
but this time things would be different.
I would let him coil
in the top of that fallen pine,
his hourglass markings dark as death,
and against everything I've ever been taught,
would step around him,
no rock, no stick, no gun,
just staying alive in Mississippi.

◆ ◆ ◆

III. Mississippi Scrapbook

◆ ◆ ◆

*We lived close to the rhythms of
life in Mississippi. We knew when
the babies were born. We knew
who was sick and who was dying.
We hunted and fished, we played
the games we taught ourselves, we
explored the woods and found secret
places. And in the center of it all
was the family and the community
and the church. The photographs
in this section capture and share
some of those rhythms. At left, Rev.
Ewart A. and Lola Mae Autry and
son Jerry, who died when he was 17.
At right, Martha Lynn Autry (now
Crawford) with older brother Jerry
and their catch. Below, Ewart, the
twins Martha Lynn and Lanny, and
Jimmy (the author) in the big poplar
tree deep in the woods*

We called it grabblin', and big fish were the reward, but grabblin' was as much a social event and a boy's rite of passage as anything else. When threatened, a catfish will make a rumbling sound, and the man who hears him will call, "I hear him thundering!" At right, a group of men probe a large drift of logs in the river-a sure bedding place for the big fish. But will there be a fish, or a snake, or a snapping turtle? At left, Martha Lynn and a neighbor and a prize fish. Below, three "good old boys," including Uncle Everson Autry (center). Out of the river the fish is helpless, but in chest-deep water he could drown any man foolish enough to put a hand in that mouth.

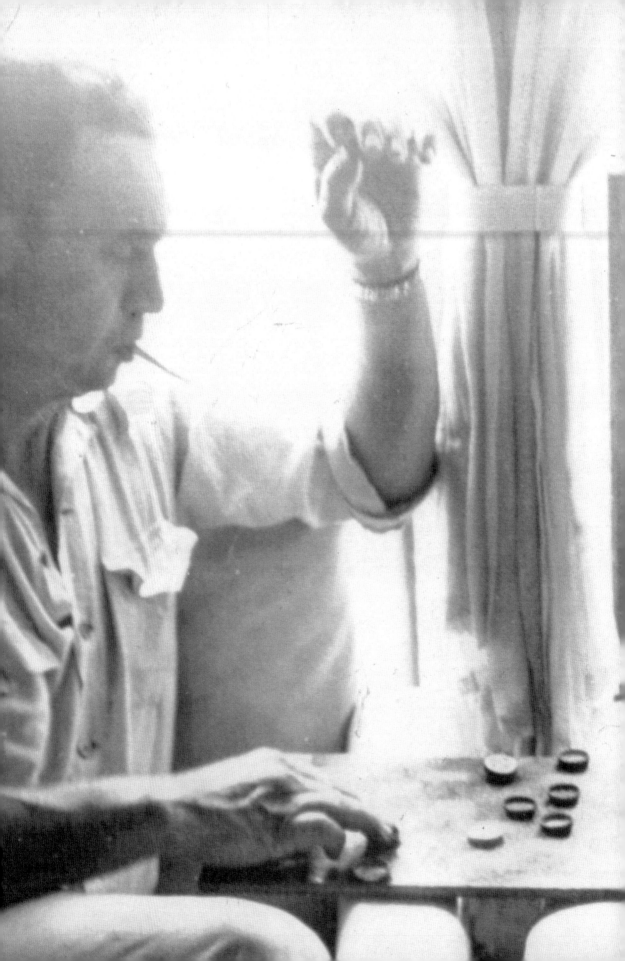

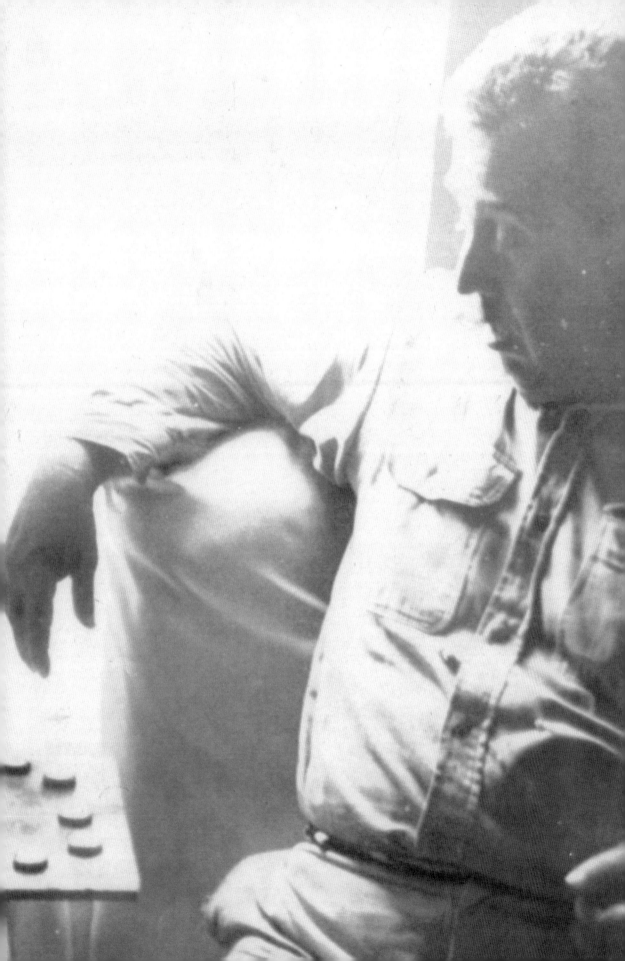

Then there was plain old fishing, with poles, lines, hooks, and bait. At left, Lanny and a "grinnell." Below, Ewart and a big snapper. At right, a neighbor wading out among the fish.

Animals, even insects, were valuable everyday parts of our lives. We hunted with dogs and plowed with mules. In turn we cared for their needs, and they became like members of the family. At left, Lanny with a faithful foxhound; Below, Jerry and Jimmy in a sled drawn by old Joe. At right, Lanny and Martha Lynn in the excitement of a "Betsy Bug Chariot Race" -match boxes pulled by bugs in harnesses of thread.

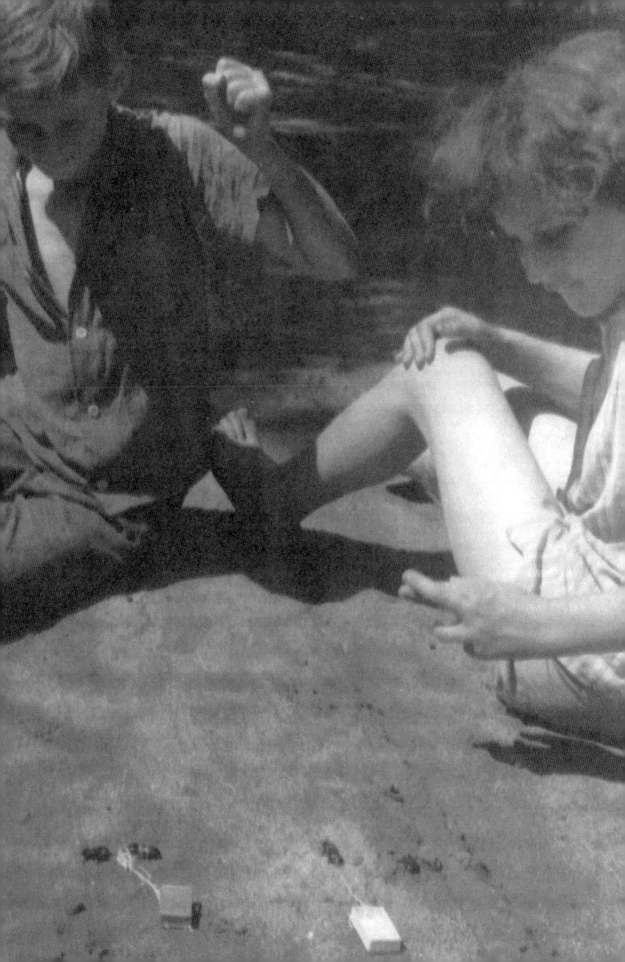

Political campaigns were more benign and considerably more entertaining in those days. The people gave the candidates time and a place to visit. While the "gossip center" at left was done in good humor, the people came to listen seriously-though some speeches, even then, were dull enough to make the babies sleep. Below, men and boys sit at Abel's store, practicing the lost art of watching the cars go by.

The church was the center of the community in earlier years and was the source of its own special stories. At left is Pine Grove Church where, as the story was often told, a Yankee patrol came and, leaving weapons outside, worshipped with the children and old people who made up the congregation during the war. In this cemetery are Civil War graves still clearly marked. Below, Ewart Autry; long time pastor of Pine Grove; in the background is a picture of his father, Rev. James A. Autry; also pastor of Pine Grove in the early years of the 20th century. At right, Ewart baptizes Jerry; his son, in the Tippah River.

Hunting meant food first, sport second. The rule in most families was "kill to eat, and eat what you kill," the only exceptions being poisonous snakes and varmints that preyed on chickens and small livestock. Above, Jerry (at left) and Lanny (second from right) and friends at the end of a rabbit hunt. At right, a proud Cousin Douglas Autry and his buck. At left, a possum up a tree.

From the time people first cut roads through the woods of north Mississippi or cleared a path for fences or power lines, the rains, with no undergrowth to slow the water, would wash away the soil. We thought kudzu would stop all that. To some extent it did, but nothing has been able to stop the kudzu. It smothers out thousands of acres of trees every year, and as it grows and climbs every thing in its path, it takes on eerie shapes, as in the photo at left. Below, it reclaims for nature an abandoned house. At right, a tree deep in the Autry woods, dubbed by Ewart as "nature's totem pole."

No one bought bait from a handy bait shop. There were three ways to get it: 1) catch insects like crickets or cockroaches or grass-hoppers; 2) dig for worms or grubs or "ground puppies" (salaman-ders), or 3) seine for small fish or crawfish or other water creatures. Here, seining for bait in Autry Creek are Jerry, Lanny, Martha Lynn, and Ewart.

The dramatic photograph at right is of an Autry friend and neighbor and hunting companion, Mr. C. A. Falkner, with his "Judas crow," which he trained to call other crows. When they came, Mr. CA. would shoot them.

At left, Ewart measures a big poplar tree, one of the few not cut years ago for lumber.

Below, the Tippah River, around which much life flowed. We fished in it, grabbled in it, swam in it, baptized in it, picnicked on its banks. We planted crops in the fields, which the river, with disheartening frequency, would then flood and ruin. The channeling of the Tippah stopped the regular floods and put much land into crop production-but it also put an end to the river's central role in our lives.

III. Paying
Attention

◆ ◆ ◆

Photograph by Sally Pederson

New Birth
for Sally
Spring, 1984

From her sure knowledge
that everything would come out all right,
things began to come out all right,
out through the present day horrors,
through my fears and loss and grief,
through the demons lurking around everything I do.

As if directly from that optimism,
Ronald came unconcerned into the cold and light,
no longer surrounded by the sounds of Sally's life,
but sliding easily into the doctor's bloody hands
then snuggling back onto his mother's warmth,
none of his father's wailing against the world,
none of that waiting for the next shoe to fall.

And I count toes and fingers
and check his little penis
and touch the soft spot on his head
and watch the doctor probe and squeeze,
not believing everything came out all right.

Later I wonder how these years have come
from pain to death to pain to life
to what next?
A baby babbling in the backpack,
a mother walking her healthy pace,
a dog trailing behind,
and me holding on,
through the neighborhood, through everything,
with each day
one by one
coming out all right.

◆ ◆ ◆

On Paying Attention

There came a time in my volunteer life
when I began to give in
to the seductions of righteousness
and to think of my work as a sacrifice
for the good of others.
I would make schedules no one should try
so that people would ask
how it was possible for one man to do so much.
It was a time of three speeches
and three cities
in one day,
and in all the scurrying
I did not want the delay
of a restroom conversation
with a hesitant little man
in a cheap new suit.
I needed a quick pee, five minutes to think,
and two minutes to get to the podium.
But there he was,
with the side effects I knew so well,
the puffy cheeks, the swollen gums
as he smiled and told me he had a job now
and hadn't had a seizure in six months.
I gave him the quick back pat and the smile,
never expecting to see him again.
But he sat in the front row
and smiled a greeting when I rose to speak,
the dignitary from the national office,
bringing word from Washington,
the National Commission,
the Hill, the White House.
He smiled too often
and over-nodded and made too much of his notes,
clicking his pen and turning pages,
back and forth,
as if studying what he'd written.
When our eyes met he smiled and nodded,
another guy, I thought, who wants people

to think he knows the speaker.
So I avoided looking at him
until he shuffled, crossed his legs,
and stretched them in front of him.
When I saw the soles of his shoes,
slightly soiled, less than a day worn,
I realized he had bought the suit and shoes
just for this meeting,
just to hear a speech squeezed
into an afternoon between two other cities.
He had looked forward to it,
planned for it,
put new job money into it,
and would make notes
so that he could remember always
what the important man came to teach.

But the lesson was mine to learn–
about sacrifice
and counting blessings,
about patience
and paying attention to teachers
wherever I find them.

◆ ◆ ◆

Airport Scene I.

She had country girl written all over her,
except on her T-shirt
which said "I'm terrific,"
but I know she never said terrific
until she came to the city
and went to secretary school
and learned to dress and make up
then got a job
and tried to be terrific
enough to marry a new salesman
now getting off a plane
on Friday night,
too tired for the baby on her hip
and wondering if his wife's body
will ever be terrific again.

◆ ◆ ◆

Airport Scene II.

It used to be train stations
but now it's airports,
the core sample of humanity,
rushing always and waiting,
crying hellos and goodbyes.
Think about that,
how high and fast they go,
machines full of people,
miracle rays guiding them everywhere on earth,
billions of dollars of invisible signals
bringing the people down safely
so they can rush and wait
and cry their hellos and goodbyes,
just like in the train stations.

◆ ◆ ◆

Airport Scene III.

I know a traveler in a hurry,
always fidgeting in the rampway,
who wants to paint a red line
on the floor at every gate
and announce "No hugging or kissing
before you reach the red line"
so other people,
especially him,
won't be delayed by all that affection.

◆ ◆ ◆

Airport Scene IV.

Infants they say have a special filter
that shuts down the hearing
when the world gets too loud,
letting them sleep through
jack hammers or rock and roll,
an enviable gift, I think,
rushing through an airport,
but reserved for infants
because they would not be able
to deal with the noise,
and would scream
at the engines
and metal announcements
and whistles and horns.

But when the body grows
we hear it all
whether we can deal with it or not,
a random thought,
seeing a retarded woman in the crosswalk,
amidst the horns and whistles and yells,
her father at her side,
her eyes moving without focus,
her body jerking against the noise,
like a shot rabbit against the pellets,
but the father squeezing and patting,
his head close,
pouring his "okay" and "good" and "almost there"
into her ear,
love filtering the noise.

◆ ◆ ◆

Widow

She told the children
they didn't have to keep going to the same church,
they could take their children to a bigger church,
with a gym and a pool,
not reminding them their father was still
fertilizing the azaleas
where he had been scattered,
white dust on a rainy day,
drifting under the black umbrellas
after we dug our hands into the urn
and broadcast him
like seed
among the flowers
then walked to the cars
and noticed him
like talcum
on our shoes and around our cuffs,
and later found he had come home with us,
under our fingernails,
then before supper
scrubbed with those little stiff bristle brushes
and tried to wash him away.

◆ ◆ ◆

Listening To Old Wounds

A man I love is going crazy
they say,
but he says it's only his hearing.

> *Get a hearing aid*, I say

and he says,

> *Then people shout at you.*

And I say,

> *I am shouting.*

He knows the truth
but tells me he used to have good ears,

> *I could hear a whine on the line*
> *a hundred yards away.*
> *Knew just which pole to climb.*

and that the Japs ruined his hearing
in New Guinea,
the night they parachuted
right on top of his unit,
silent among the foxholes,
all of them lost in the dark,
shouting passwords and trusting no one.

> *I had to listen too hard*
> *that night. A twig cracking.*
> *Anything.*

After the fighting he sat
for weeks
pounding an Australian coin with
a soup spoon
until the coin became a ring

which he sent me,
too big then
but which I wore for years.
Now he doesn't remember the ring,
and when I mention it
he cocks his head and squints,
as if listening for the memory,
but he hears only
"them damn jabbering yellow monkeys"
drifting above him,

> *They didn't know*
> *we were down there and we couldn't tell*
> *where the voices were coming from.*

then dropping among his buddies,
the shooting and screaming,
the silence,
life depending on his ears.

I can understand why they say
he's going crazy.
It has something to do with all the sounds,
heartbeats, footsteps, breathing,
out there somewhere,
who knows how far away,
but still listened for–
still listened for.

◆ ◆ ◆

Madrap**
for Jimmy

This is a place of daily miracles
where strangers sit in circles
and discover the lost language of love,
putting themselves back together,
fitting tears and anger and pain
like puzzle pieces
until their stories make sense again.

◆ ◆ ◆

**
Mercy Alcohol and Drog Rehabilitation Program, MA.D.R.P.,
pronounced "Madrap" by those in the program

Hospital Visits

Under my arm is a blue folder
stuffed with everything I could ever learn
about booze and dope
except how to feel when
sitting in a circle with other children
it comes his tum and he says
"I'm Jim, an alcoholic and drug addict."

Next to me in the elevator is a couple with a pillow
for sitting on the floor
in a circle with other couples
learning to strain and grunt and breathe
another child into birth.

In the slow and acrid elevator
I want to tell them everything
about how it never ends,
being a parent,
about how it transforms you forever,
beyond celebration or pain or death.

But this is not the time or place
for a born again father to make his speech,
so I say "good luck"
and pray safe deliverance for us all.

◆ ◆ ◆

Baptism

There's something about this,
about putting the people under the water
and raising them up
in the name of the Father, the Son, and the Holy Ghost,
something that makes the people cry,
that makes them want to want
everything to be all right,
that makes them want to leave this place
and be better,
to immerse themselves in their lives
and somehow be washed clean
of all the things they think
they should not have done
and should not still want to do.
That's it.
Not the other stuff,
the star in the east,
the treasures in heaven,
or any of the old stories.
Not even life after death.
It is only to be new again.

◆ ◆ ◆

Present Day Horrors

The present day horrors
would be bad enough in themselves,
abstractly,
but it's the little scenes of desperation and despair
playing through everything
that finally get us:
A kleenex full of phlegm

> *Save that. Don't throw it away.*
> (I won't.)
> *They don't believe I cough up stuff.*
> *Save it. Show them.*
> (I will.)

And the nurse comes and I give it to her
with all the urgency I can feign

> *See?*
> *They said there was nothing there.*

And he grins and nods
knowing they will believe him now.

Later I see a tiny light of recognition
after the lung collapses and I come
in the midst of the struggle
wondering how and when it will end
watching that wild stare over the respirator mask
seeing all the energy go with every breath,
none to spare for the hello nod,
only enough for one more breath,
and one more.

Then someone says

> *When the eyes get dry it's over.*

and I wonder what that means

watching the eyes dryer and dryer
until something very small changes
and I think

> *Shit he's not here now.*
> *He's not staying for this part.*

the spaces between breaths growing
until that's all there is.

And that last space fills with memories
of little struggles in the middle of the night,
of incoherent sentences
like "oh why now pee"
and I hold his penis and point it into the bedpan
as he used to hold mine those years ago
when he was the adult and I was the child.
And he is embarrassed
and I am embarrassed for him
but we smile,
a last signal that after all this
we're still together
through these little scenes,
through the phlegm
and urine and blood and oxygen
and hypos and IVs,
through every pun and every game
and every old joke,
right up to the lung-crushing eye-drying end .

◆ ◆ ◆

The Wig

It was as if he had not even tried
for a match,
the way the ads promise,
using real human hair
to match what was there before,
and we didn't know what to say
when he limped into the office,
then he laughed,
"Hell, with the doctor bills,
who can afford a decent rug?"
and we realized it was his last big joke.
One day the wig was short, another long,
then he changed colors,
then blacked a tooth,
"always clowning," we would say later,
shaking our heads and smiling,
"right up to the end."
But as usual we missed the point,
about how people pay more attention to a clown
than to a dying man.

◆ ◆ ◆

Camping Memories

Surrounded by a deep and warm night
we breathed into each other's hair.
Life moved around us and between us,
creatures and feelings waked and stirred
making quiet and simple sounds.
There were no predators.
Reptiles did not bite
and insects did not sting.

◆ ◆ ◆

In John Maguire's Garden
Claremont, May 15, 1988

Very formal in places
because some people need the predictability,
this garden still has wild spots which draw me,
like a raucous chorus of Amazing Grace
late after some distinguished dinner,
or an eyebrow twisting upward
below a mortar board,
unexpected, distracting, beyond cultivation.

Some might hurry to prune the overgrown places,
to soften the surprise
of coming upon life so extravagant
that it outblooms the boundaries.
But not me, John,
not me.
I believe the gardener knew what he was doing.

◆ ◆ ◆

Reminiscence At Toul
July 18, 1987

Thirty years ago
on New Year's eve
drunk on French champagne
we shot bottle rockets
from the windows
of Hank and Willi's
rented chateau overlooking Nancy.

It sounds so worldly
which is how we wanted to think of ourselves,
but Lord, we were just children,
sent by the government to fly airplanes
and to save western Europe
from World War III.

We thought we had all the important things
still left to do
and were just playing at importance
for the time being.
It never occurred to us,
living in our community of friends,
having first babies,
seeing husbands die,
helping young widows pack to go home,
that we had already started the important things.
What could we have been thinking,
or perhaps it's how could we have known
that times get no better,
that important things come without background music,
that life is largely a matter of paying attention.

◆ ◆ ◆

Tannois

for Adam Growald
July 21, 1987, aboard The Princess

At the *lavois*
down the hill from her house
she tells about the day
she saved the Americans from the rain,
two men, two women, and a child,
un petit garcon,
nineteen months old the mother said,
on bicycles in the rain,
and she tells how they came in
and how they loved her dog and cats and doves.
It was in the summer of 1987
and they came on bicycles
from a boat on the canal,
in the rain,
and stopped under her eaves
and she invited them in.
And the others listen,
having heard it before,
and shake their heads
about Americans riding bicycles in the rain.

How large it seemed to her
in the smallness of her kitchen
with its backless chairs and curtainless windows,
in the smallness of her village,
where foreigners come through,
sometimes in tanks and sometimes on bicycles,
sometimes to make war
and sometimes to come in out of the rain.

Years from now a boy will look at a snapshot.
His mother will say,
your Uncle Jim took this the day
we got caught in the rain,
and this old French lady,
see her in the shadows there,
invited us into her home.
The boy will smile at the picture,
but he can never believe
that in a village in France,
among old ladies gathered at the *lavois*,
there still is talk of how
their friend once saved the Americans from the rain.

◆ ◆ ◆

Life In America

There's a line I want to use,
see?
in a poem I want to write,
okay?
Now don't groan or roll your eyes.
Give me a break.
I mean, hey, give it a chance
to grow on you,
okay?
It's a line I thought of,
watching some guys after a golf game
drinking in the club house
and slapping cards on the table
and checking their watches and saying
like, you know; "oh hell,
about time to go home or my old lady'll
give me a load of shit."
This line is about those guys
plus a lot of other people,
let me tell you,
people in loud dance places,
standing around the floor,
checking out the action,
if you know what I mean.
And people in bowling alleys,
okay?
yelling at the pins and each other.
This line,
and believe me, I wrote it myself,
I swear I never heard it before,
this line is about all those people I see
and not just those,
others,
at restaurants and ball games
and even at church.
It's a line about how they act
and in a way it's a line about America.
But hey, I don't want to get too heavy,

you know?
I just want to say this one little line
and let you take it from there,
okay?
Hey look, seriously, the line is
(are you ready for this?)
"living lives of boisterous desperation."
Lives of boisterous desperation.
How about that?
Not *quiet* desperation, like the other guy wrote
about another time and another place,
but *boisterous* desperation.
Get it?
Get it?
Sure you do.

◆ ◆ ◆

The Story Of The Beginning
Of The End Of The World

It was a time when many people had the answers.
Some sold the answers
to other people who came
on weekends to listen and
nod and hug each other and
sometimes scream and sometimes
take off their clothes and
always say "thank you for sharing."

Some sold the answers
in books about feeling better and
taking charge of your life and
walking a new path and
discovering many zones and spots
you never knew you had
in your head or on your body.

Some sold the answers
in church with quotations about
giving and receiving and
which one is always better and
warnings about finding the answers in
books or from false prophets
who abounded in times like these.

Some sold the answers
in business schools and in stock markets,
in union halls and in capitals of government
and, for those of lesser means,
in blind alleys and back stairways
and places where other people
wouldn't even think to look for the answers.

◆ ◆ ◆

Leo

He threw water on my motorcycle's one sparkplug
so I wouldn't be able to leave him,
so I would have to stay,
his buddy,
and play in the back yard,
the only place he was allowed to go.

Early before anyone was up
he would fill a tumbler with tap water
then sneak out the front door
of his side of the duplex
and tiptoe to where the Harley 125 was chained
and pour a little puddle around the plug.

Later, late and frustrated,
drying the plug, grease on my hands,
I would yell at him

> *Goddammit, Leo, you're making me late*
> *I've got to go to school.*

and sometimes chase him and pretend
I was going to hit him.
But he would only repeat what he said
every morning of every day of every year
we lived in that duplex

> *You Leo's buddy*
> *Play with Leo now.*

Leo would stand,
his big droopy frame shutting out the light
from the back screen door,
and watch mother cook.

> *Rufe play with Leo?*

His breathing was noisy and he sometimes drooled

and his eyes looked in different directions.
Mother would say "that big dumb thing
scares me and I wish they'd keep him
off the back porch,"
and I would say "if he's so dumb
how does he know to ground out my sparkplug."

We knew his age and his mind's age
and we knew they'd didn't match,
but we didn't know anything else
except he was Italian
and his big family kept him there with them,
in the duplex,
and they had barbecues in the backyard
and drank beer and laughed with each other,
and that Leo played on the ground
with the other children
like a big pet, I thought.
And they all seemed happy enough.

I hadn't thought about Leo in years, of course,
until just the other day,
just after the tests were in,
just after the pediatrician
in his I am your friend voice
said something to us like,
"Well, he'll never go to Harvard Medical School,
but he'll be very functional
and will be able to do a lot of things."

Later, I wondered if that meant things like
ground out a sparkplug with a glass of water
or play the family pet
with children a third his age.

And I thought,
sometimes God makes you write things on the blackboard
a thousand times.

◆ ◆ ◆

Distractions

It was a matter of distraction;
I could not hear my baby sons,
those struggling years ago,
in a trailer or an apartment
or old house where I thought
money was the problem
and did not want to be distracted
by the babbling of children.
Or it could have been the constrictions,
of a trailer, an apartment, an old house, a cockpit
or an office with two other people
and no way to stand out
but to put my head down and work
so hard I could not afford
to be constricted by children.

But this is not the same old cry of guilt,
the if-only-I-had-another-chance,
because after all these years
a chance came,
another son,
this time with me ready to listen.
But he is distracted,
something about constrictions in his brain
making him busy inside himself,
with so much to do
that he talks to himself
more than to me,
and every day I try to persuade him
to live in this world
and to let me know he's with me
if only from time to time.

◆ ◆ ◆

Poet's Prayer

If I write another poem
let it be about love,
not the crazy love
we all start out writing about
but the love that keeps us sane,
the love that pain reveals
at a funeral
or when the doctor says what we don't want to hear;
the love that men won't talk about,
of work, of games, of one another;
the love of divorced people
when they find their way back to marriage;
the love of an old family place
when the generations gather there;
the love of old friends
who realize they're the only ones left;
and the love of children,
not only when they're smiling or sleeping
or clean or straight or strong or smart,
but when they are none of those things
and need more love than anyone can give,
and cannot even recognize the love they get.

◆ ◆ ◆

Matters Of The Heart
(On the Lear, after learning of a
blocked coronary artery, 4/20/80)

What makes the heart stop?

> On the Lear the heart stops
> when the noise stops
> or the CAT strikes.

What about the flatbed truck?

> Then too,
> Chigger trying to jump the ditch
> behind the road machine
> or hit it,
> on the way to Wolf River
> where the yellow water tried to suck me under.

And the motorcycle?

> Yes, I twisted the handlebar
> pushing myself at the heart's edge
> with the fear in seconds,
> spinning and tumbling on the muddy road.

What then of the cancer?

> It did not happen to me.

Didn't it?

> It was the heart, remember?

But wasn't your heart connected to his cancer?

> And to many things.

So what really makes the heart stop?

> No one knows,
> but I know this:
> it practices and practices.

◆ ◆ ◆

Christmas In New York

Don't let *Adeste Fideles* near a tenor sax
or else
some gaunt music major
will beat it to death for tuition.
At Bloomie's the Salvation Army lady
carols on a baritone horn,
and a fey young man listens,
tiny jingle bells in a pierced ear.
On the church steps the Fifth Avenue Four
urge themselves onward
through the *Saints*,
from the music stamped
''Property of Juilliard,''
perfectly,
which is not how it is to be played.

Could I take my sax
and fake it through Christmas on a corner?
Not the music but the rest of it,
the youth
the cold
the needs
the hope
the feeling
it hasn't passed me by,
or vice versa?

◆ ◆ ◆

Homeless Saxophonist

I can tell from his riffs
he is not on Lexington Avenue,
leaning against Grand Central,
his fingers our only proof he's still alive.
We are here,
stepping around his feet,
pushing our way uptown,
his notes wild against the taxi horns.
But he is not playing where we are;
he is in another place,
a dark place small and crowded,
where people are smiling and shaking their heads
in that funny way real jazz fans have,
and there is a bass
and drums
and piano,
always with him, steady as dirt,
chords leading to just where he wants his sax to take him,
farther away still,
to a place he has not yet been
but will know the first time he feels it.

◆ ◆ ◆

Why Men Fly

We sat around waiting
to see who had lit up the desert,
each of us with somebody
we did not want it to be,
burning out there,
coyotes and pack rats,
bright-eyed by the fire,
running jumping onto and around
rags of hot metal
scattered a mile,
nibbling perhaps at the odd chunks of meat.

All of us wondered the same thing
as each number landed,

> *Apache four two is in*
> *Apache one eight is in*

as each head-shaking, wet-suited man
came in counting the chairs,
checking each face for the missing one.

We did not know that melodrama
worked against us
until a cajun boy hit his fist
on the table and sobbed,
"Why didn't they get out?"
And one of the instructors
hand-picked a bunch of us into another room
and said
"Anybody who can't take this without crying
better quit now."
Then as we tried variations on stony faced,
he said,
"After all, if flying were safe,
why the hell do it?"

◆ ◆ ◆

Flying Safety Lesson

They said it was a lesson
about oxygen management,
then came a tape of radio talk,
an incident they called it,
involving a flight of four F-100s
from the States to Spain
with a stop in the Azores,
beginning with those voices you've heard
in the flying movies,

> "Check in, Red Four."
> "Roger."
> The Roger doesn't sound right,
> slurred,
> so the leader says "Oxygen check,"
> but by then it is already too late,
> and Red Four mumbles.

We knew why they wanted us to hear the tape,
something about fear,
about checking oxygen,
about things not to do
like starve our brains and dive into the sea,
old stuff we knew already.
But the mumble
made our necks tingle,
weeks later listening.

> The leader says, "Three, check out Red Four."
> Red Four says nothing,
> then Red Three shouts,
> "Pull up, Red Four, you're diving.
> Pull up, pull up."

We did not look at one another
but picked at our fingernails
or doodled or stared at the tape player.
Later we would discuss oxygen management
and safety checks
and all the routines that became so routine
between the Azores and Spain
that they didn't get done.

Then comes the radar controller's voice,
steady, commanding,
"Red Four, this is Racecar Radar,
turn heading one three five degrees,"
then scared,
"Sir... Red Four Sir...please
tum right...now...heading one four zero degrees."
Then Red Three drops the call sign,
"Bob, please listen to me,
pull up, level your wings,
look at me, wave, give me a sign,
say something."

Then the mumble,
trying hard we thought,
but too late the Flight Surgeon told the class,
"His brain was gone by that time, Gentlemen."

Now the tape plays a lot of silence.
Red Three says, "Bob, please pull up,
pull back on the stick, ease back on the stick."
And the radar man asks "Altitude?"
And Red Three says, "five thousand and descending,"
and the radar man says
"Red Four...sir...please turn right...
please pull up."
And Red Three says,
his voice breaking at the edges,
"Bob look at me, wave, pull up."
Silence,
a shout, "No Bob, pull up, pull up."
More silence.
"Too late, too late."
And the radar man gives the coordinates
and the tape shuts off.

I don't remember the words the instructors chose
to restate the obvious,
but I remember the lesson they never intended,
about how technology fails
and humanity is the only thing left,
which sometimes is not enough.

◆ ◆ ◆

Examining The Wreckage

I am drawn to plane crashes.
I read about them,
every detail,
and try to figure out what happened
and what the pilot did wrong,
which is only a way of wondering what I would have done.

And of course I would have done it right,
have analyzed the problem,
the sputtering engine,
the heavy controls,
the failed generator,
and I would have gotten down okay,
and I would never have flown in that weather,
and I would have watched for ice,
and I would have turned back,
and I would never have gone near that thunderstorm
or flown those mountains at night
or taken a single engine over water
or any of those dumb things
other pilots do every day.

But when I think about the pilot years
I remember things done wrong:
an aileron roll too close to the ground,
a foggy landing I should not have tried,
a thunderstorm full of hail
like the sound of a thousand hammers,
a failed drag chute, a blown tire
and a bomb under the wing.
All that without a crash.

At this point I should make a metaphor
about life and flying,
but flying is easier than life.
When a plane crashes,
I can go there and know
that I am not in the wreckage.

◆ ◆ ◆

Jeopardy

I

How many times have I died?
At least once on the motorcycle,
with Jack Spencer on the back,
the unexpected cars
and the boy on the bicycle
and nothing to do but skid and hope.
Or run off the road
by the Cadillac passing on the hill
outside Holly Springs.
And certainly in the F-86
over the cotton fields below Rabat
with Dickie on the radio

Jesus, Cowboy, pull up before you roll!

(Think of that,
of all the hoeing and picking,
of all the sun hot hours in cotton fields,
to hang my wing
and tumble into pieces
on some foreigner's cotton
ten thousand miles from my people's land.)

And in the fog at Wethersfield
in an Englishman's pasture
with sheep like gray boulders
in a wash of green
only a hundred yards from the runway
but far enough that all I could say
was Oh Shit.

And in the whistling silence
of a dead engine.
And in a thunderstorm
that rolled back and wrinkled the metal skin
like an old time cigarette paper.

And in a hundred things I didn't even know about.

II

There are courts of inquiry somewhere,
accident investigators piecing it together.
There are coroners,
there are undertakers trying to make me
look okay after all.
There are caskets shipped back
filled with rubber sacks
not nearly full enough.
There are honor guards clicking their heels
and firing rifles in country cemeteries.
There are proud mothers
and wet-eyed widows
and children with pictures for fathers.

III

But through all those deaths,
I am here,
still and again,
with at least one to go,
and the only thing changed
is the limb I am out on.

◆ ◆ ◆

ABOUT THE AUTHOR

James A. Autry (b. March 8, 1933), a former Fortune 500 executive, is the author of fourteen books, a poet and consultant whose work has had a significant influence on leadership thinking. His book, Love and Profit, The Art of Caring Leadership, a collection of essays and poetry, won the prestigious Johnson, Smith & Knisely Award as the book which had the most impact on executive thinking in 1992. Love and Profit also has been published in Japanese, Swedish, Chinese, Spanish, and Russian, and is still in print in paperback.

In addition, Autry has written the introductions to several books, and his writings have appeared in many anthologies and magazines. In 1991 the Kentucky Poetry Review published a special James A. Autry issue. He is a founder of the Des Moines National Poetry Festival.

He received considerable national attention when he was one of the poets featured on Bill Moyers' special series, "The Power of the Word." Moyers featured him again in 2012 on Moyers & Company on PBS. Garrison Keillor has featured his work on "The Writer's Corner" on public radio. Autry is also featured in three videos, "Love and Profit," which won a "Telly" award, "Life and Work," and "Spirit at Work." In 1998 he received the Lifetime Achievement Award for Service to the Humanities from Iowa Humanities Board and Foundation. He was also the founding chair of the Claremont Graduate University's Humanities Center Board of Visitors.

Autry was named a Distinguished Alumnus of the University of Mississippi and was elected to the Alumni Hall of Fame. He fulfilled his military service as a jet fighter pilot in Europe during the Cold War and rose to the rank of Major in the Iowa Air National Guard.

Before taking early retirement in 1991 to pursue his present career, Autry was Senior Vice President and President of the Meredith Group, at the time a 500 million dollar magazine publishing operation with over 900 employees.

Autry lives in Des Moines, Iowa, with his wife Sally Pederson, the former Lieutenant Governor of Iowa.